THE SWEET ROASTING TIN

ONE TIN CAKES, COOKIES & BAKES

FOR TIM,
WITH LOVE

THE SWEET ROASTING TIN

ONE TIN CAKES, COOKIES & BAKES

RUKMINI IYER

CONTENTS

INTRODUCTION

While I've paused my occasional secret daydream of opening a cake shop (which now has a marble-topped bar and extensive wine list, along with a savoury menu), the easy, one-tin cakes and bakes in this book are what you'd find in my imaginary shop and real-life kitchen. I've broadened the definition of 'one-tin' to include muffin tins, cupcake tins and baking trays for cookies – because why limit yourself to one shape of sweet thing? (The only shape I wish I'd included was the mini dinosaur tins for dinosaur-shaped cakes, but perhaps that's for another book.)

I've loved baking for as long as I can remember: it started with my mother, and a really good collection of cookbooks. At first, it was the brightly coloured ones aimed at children, from which we made flapjacks, butterfly and chocolate cakes (decorated with chocolate buttons), graduating not very long afterwards to a pale-pink-macaron-coloured *Patisserie* book, part of the Time-Life series. As a child, I began reading it obsessively over breakfast: the step-by-step photographs showed the reader how to whisk egg white and sugar into cloud-like meringues, with pages on melting and dipping chocolate and shaping it into curls, and guides to making your own piping bags and creating filigree decorations – as entrancing as any picture book. Along with a book on cake decorating (rolling a cake covered in green buttercream through a tray of desiccated coconut to create a grassy effect) and a Cadbury book of baking (featuring elaborate chocolate castles with biscuit trellis-work), it's fair to say that I read about cakes almost as often as I ate them.

Happily, the things we actually made at home were much simpler, and all the nicer for it. Childhood highlights included home-made doughnuts, laced with cardamom, my mother's pineapple upside-down cake and orange chocolate chip steamed puddings (both of which made their way into *The Roasting Tin*), and the coconut burfi which you will find on page 218. Much as I still enjoy looking at photographs and how-to videos of elaborately iced and decorated cakes, my preference when baking or eating is still with those that are simple to put together and minimally adorned.

With icing or without, the premise of this baking book is simple: after all the reading and experimenting that I have done, I am convinced that for every category of baking – a loaf cake, a cupcake, a cookie, a bread and butter pudding – there is one very simple recipe template, from which you can make multiple variations for an almost infinite variety of flavours and textures. Take a cake, one of the easiest things you can make. As I explain in more detail on page 15, for a basic cake you use equal quantities by weight of flour, butter, sugar and eggs. But if all you need is equal weights per category, then you can theoretically swap the butter for olive oil, or the flour for ground almonds, the caster sugar for soft dark brown sugar, or the eggs for mashed banana and peanut butter, and come up with a cake that is subtly different each time. While I really don't recommend making all these changes at once (I found this out the hard way), the gentle variations on the template within each chapter will I hope demonstrate that even if you find baking a little daunting, you only have to get a recipe right once before a whole array of flavour combinations is at your disposal.

The baking book that has inspired me most is undoubtedly Nigella's *How to be a Domestic Goddess*, which I read as absolute gospel as a teenager, and still consider to be so. Feeling that I must have the wherewithal to make a batch of cakes at a minute's notice is so deeply ingrained that even as a student I was never without flour, butter, sugar and eggs. The idea that you can create anything from a light, fluffy sponge to a melt-in-the-mouth pudding or tinful of cookies from such simple ingredients never fails to amaze me: it feels like very little effort, and time, for such a pleasing result. And as such the recipes fit perfectly into my Roasting Tin mantra of 'minimum effort, maximum return' cooking – a little light stirring, get your ingredients in a (muffin, loaf or cake) tin, and let the oven do the work.

VEGAN, GLUTEN-FREE & DIABETIC-FRIENDLY RECIPES IN THIS BOOK

Of course, it's not just the flavours that you're altering when you swap out ingredients in the recipe templates in this book. For as long as I can remember, my mother has tinkered with gluten-free scone or cake recipes to cater for a coeliac friend or visitor, and more recently has been baking without sugar for my father, who is diabetic. I am not an expert on vegan baking, but my all-time favourite banana bread and cookie recipes happen to be naturally vegan, and so I've applied the principles from those so you can easily veganise other recipes in this book should you wish. (Because I believe it to be the best recipe, inadvertently all the cookies in the book are vegan.) Similarly, when testing chocolate brownie recipes, I found that those made with ground almonds – which I would initially have labelled the gluten-free option – were far better in their own right than those made with flour, and so almost the entire brownie chapter of this book is incidentally gluten-free. Remember to always check the labels on ingredients, including baking powder and chocolate, to ensure they're gluten-free, if you need them to be.

If, like my mother and me, you've got someone in your life who loves cake and can't eat it because they're diabetic, I wanted there to be recipes in this book that you could easily convert to be diabetic-friendly. But as diabetic baking is a specialist area, I've worked with nutritionist Jennifer Martin on the recipes in this book to determine which ones are easily adaptable with date syrup or xylitol, our preferred sugar substitutes. You'll find a table on page 225 so you can determine the approximate level of carbohydrates of which are sugars for each of the suitable recipes and make your own assessment. If you are making the diabetic substitutions for a recipe, be sure to check the table for the specific diabetic-friendly portion sizes for each. Please check the dietary suitability of these recipes with your GP if in any doubt (and see page 221 for more information on obtaining medical advice if necessary).

For an at-a-glance look at which recipes in the book are naturally vegan/gluten-free/suitable for diabetics, and which ones can be easily made so with a quick ingredient swap, see pages 222–224.

TRAYBAKES

CHERRY & ALMOND

CHOCOLATE -LIME TRUFFLE

COCONUT & MANGO YOGURT

MARMALADE COFFEE

ORANGE & HAZELNUT

APPLE & PINE NUT

SPICED CARROT & COCONUT
(GLUTEN-FREE)

TRAYBAKE CAKES

The classic formula which was taught to me by my mother, and which I think holds true for most bakers of her generation and before, is that to make a cake you need equal quantities of butter, sugar and flour in ounces, with half the amount of eggs.

So your easily memorable cake formulas are:

2oz butter, 2oz sugar, 2oz flour + 1 medium egg
4oz butter, 4oz sugar, 4oz flour + 2 medium eggs
6oz butter, 6oz sugar, 6oz flour + 3 medium eggs
8oz butter, 8oz sugar, 8oz flour + 4 medium eggs

And so on. The classic formula is 'an equal weight of butter, sugar, flour and eggs': you can see why this works, as 1 medium egg weighs 2oz.

This is all much harder to remember in grams – no one goes around muttering '170, 170, 170 – 3!' But I would venture a look at a cake tin and say, with a suitably weighty pause – 'that's a six-six-six, that is' – and then enjoy a lively debate with a similarly imperial baker as to whether one could fit an eight-eight-eight cake batter into it, or whether we should crack out two round four-four-four tins, and make a sandwich cake. And then we'd go to the counter and find there's only one egg left, so it'll have to be a two-two-two (that'll get you 12 fairy cakes, or 6 muffin-sized cupcakes).

In this traybake cake chapter, the basic formula that I'll be using is as overleaf, and one of the nicest things about having a foolproof formula is that you can then start to fool about with it. Not only is this helpful if you're vegan, gluten-free or diabetic, but if you feel experimental, you have a ready-made, controlled template within which to experiment. Fancy an olive-oil cake? No problem – just use the same weight as you would of butter. Run out of flour, but found a bag of ground almonds? It's a dry ingredient, so use the same weight as you would of flour. Chocolate cake is a fun one – instead of adding cocoa powder to the existing weight of flour, which will dry out the cake, I like to replace a good weight of the flour with cocoa powder, adding a splash of milk, as cocoa powder absorbs more moisture in a cake than flour (see page 20, chocolate-lime truffle).

To veganise: I like to replace the butter with olive or coconut oil, and each egg with one mashed banana (see opposite). You could also experiment using almond, cashew or peanut butter in place of the mashed banana.

If you're gluten-free: I find the easiest route is to replace the self-raising flour with a half-and-half mixture of ground nuts (e.g. almonds, hazelnuts or pistachios) along with a good brand of gluten-free self-raising flour (Freee from Doves Farm is my favourite). You can also experiment with gram flour, which works beautifully in a carrot cake, which is why I recommend it for the spiced carrot cake on page 30.

From kitchen experiments and discussions with experienced gluten-free bakers, we've found that it's harder to get a rise out of a gluten-free cake – in the words of my lovely editor Tamsin, using nuts in the mix is therefore a nice way to manage expectations. And this probably won't be a problem if your household is anything like mine, but gluten-free cakes are nicest eaten on the day they are made.

If you're baking for a diabetic: If the recipe uses caster sugar, you can replace it with half the quantity of xylitol: this is a natural birch sugar, and is suitable for diabetics. (Xylitol is as sweet as sugar by volume, rather than by weight, which is why you need to reduce the weight of it when replacing sugar in a recipe. If you use it in the correct quantity, you won't get the 'artificial' aftertaste that you can get with other sweeteners.)

Where a recipe uses soft light brown or soft dark brown sugar, I like to use date syrup for the rich caramel notes: as it is sugar-neutral, it is suitable for diabetics. Please consult your GP to check the suitability of these ingredients in your individual case.

BASIC TRAYBAKE CAKE

170g (6oz) softened unsalted butter
170g (6oz) sugar
(caster, golden caster,
soft light or dark brown)
3 medium free-range eggs
170g (6oz) self-raising flour
1 scant teaspoon baking powder

VEGAN TRAYBAKE CAKE

170g olive or coconut oil
130g sugar (caster,
golden caster,
soft light or dark brown)
4 medium ripe bananas, (approx. 300g) mashed
170g self-raising flour
1 scant teaspoon baking powder

GLUTEN-FREE TRAYBAKE CAKE

170g softened unsalted butter
170g soft light brown sugar
3 medium free-range eggs
100g ground almonds
75g gluten-free self-raising flour
1 teaspoon baking powder

DIABETIC-FRIENDLY TRAYBAKE CAKE

170g softened unsalted butter
85g xylitol or 170ml date syrup
3 medium free-range eggs
170g self-raising flour
1 scant teaspoon baking powder

ADDITIONAL FLAVOURINGS

coffee, chocolate
berries (strawberries, blueberries, raspberries)
orchard fruit (apples, pears, plums), which would be lovely
with ground cinnamon and ginger
exotic fruit like pineapple, which are lovely with glacé cherries

CHERRY & ALMOND CAKE

I cannot pass a bakery selling cherry and almond cakes without going in to get a slice – particularly welcome after or during an outing with the pup. For me, this is a perfect all-day cake – just make sure to use the nice bright red glacé cherries for full retro impact.

Serves: 8
Prep: 15 minutes
Cook: 30–35 minutes

170g softened unsalted butter
170g soft light brown sugar
3 medium free-range eggs
100g self-raising flour
75g ground almonds
1 teaspoon baking powder
100g glacé cherries, halved
50g flaked almonds

Preheat the oven to 160°C fan/180°C/gas 4. Whisk the butter and sugar together until smooth, then beat in the eggs one at a time.

Gently fold in the self-raising flour, ground almonds and baking powder, taking care not to overmix. Spoon the batter into a lined 20cm x 26cm roasting tin.

Scatter the glacé cherries and flaked almonds over the cake, then transfer to the oven and bake for 30–35 minutes, until firm to the touch and a skewer inserted comes out clean.

Leave the cake in the tin for 5 minutes, then gently lift it out on to a wire rack and leave to cool briefly before serving warm or at room temperature.

Any leftovers will keep well in an airtight tin in a cool room for 2–3 days.

FOR GLUTEN-FREE: substitute gluten-free flour for the ordinary flour.

CHOCOLATE-LIME TRUFFLE CAKE

This cake has a rich, lime-spiked chocolate ganache sitting over a gently lime-infused chocolate sponge – a bit like a chocolate truffle with a cake layer underneath. A very grown-up cake.

Serves: 8
Prep: 15 minutes
Cook: 25–30 minutes

170g softened unsalted butter
170g soft dark brown sugar
3 medium free-range eggs
110g self-raising flour
60g cocoa powder
1 teaspoon baking powder
1 lime, zest and juice
100ml milk

GANACHE
150ml double cream
½ lime, zest only
200g dark chocolate
　(70% cocoa solids),
　very finely chopped
A pinch of sea salt flakes

Preheat the oven to 160°C fan/180°C/gas 4. Whisk the butter and sugar together until smooth, then beat in the eggs one at a time.

Gently fold in the self-raising flour, cocoa powder and baking powder, taking care not to overmix, then stir in the lime zest and juice and the milk. Spoon the batter into a lined 20cm x 26cm roasting tin.

Transfer to the oven and bake for 25–30 minutes, until firm to the touch and a skewer inserted comes out clean.

Leave the cake in the tin for 5 minutes, then gently lift it out on to a wire rack and leave to cool completely.

For the ganache, heat the double cream and lime zest in a saucepan until just under boiling, then pour it over the chopped dark chocolate in a heatproof bowl. Let it sit for 2 minutes, then whisk vigorously with the sea salt flakes until smooth and glossy.

Spread the ganache over the chocolate cake, swirling it neatly into waves if you wish, and leave it to set before slicing and serving.

Any leftovers will keep well in an airtight tin in a cool room for 2 days.

FOR DIABETICS: replace the soft dark brown sugar with 170ml date syrup, and use diabetic-friendly dark chocolate in the topping.

COCONUT & MANGO YOGURT CAKE

I ate three slices of this cake standing up at the counter the first time it came out of the oven – it's that good. The yogurt, along with the desiccated coconut, makes this a wonderfully light sponge under the roasted mango; I'd consider serving it for breakfast.

Serves: 8
Prep: 15 minutes
Cook: 30–35 minutes

120g natural full-fat yogurt
50ml coconut oil, melted
150g soft light brown sugar
3 medium free-range eggs
120g desiccated coconut
50g plain flour
1 teaspoon baking powder
1 ripe mango, chopped
    into 1cm chunks
A small handful of coconut flakes

Preheat the oven to 160°C fan/180°C/gas 4. Whisk the yogurt, coconut oil and sugar together until smooth, then beat in the eggs one at a time.

Gently fold in the desiccated coconut, plain flour and baking powder, taking care not to overmix. Spoon the batter into a lined 20cm x 26cm roasting tin.

Scatter the chopped mango all over the batter – don't worry if it looks like a bit too much for the cake, the cake will rise up around it.

Transfer to the oven and bake for 30–35 minutes, until firm to the touch and a skewer inserted into a non-mango bit comes out clean.

Leave the cake in the tin for 5 minutes, then gently lift it out on to a wire rack and leave to cool briefly before scattering over the coconut flakes and serving warm or at room temperature.

Any leftovers should be stored in the fridge: you can gently warm the slices in the microwave as needed.

FOR GLUTEN-FREE: substitute the plain flour for a good brand of gluten-free blended flour (I like Freee plain flour from Doves Farm).

FOR DIABETICS: replace the soft light brown sugar with 70g xylitol.

MARMALADE COFFEE CAKE

Marmalade and coffee are a natural combination – one on toast, one in a mug – so I decided to combine them for another cake with a distinctly grown-up flavour. Paddington would approve.

Serves: 8
Prep: 15 minutes
Cook: 25–30 minutes

170g softened unsalted butter
120g caster sugar
100g thick-cut marmalade
3 medium free-range eggs
2 teaspoons good instant coffee
   (I like Nescafé Azera)
25ml boiling water
170g self-raising flour
1 teaspoon baking powder

SYRUP
2 teaspoons good instant coffee
25ml boiling water
50g thick-cut marmalade

Preheat the oven to 160°C fan/180°C/gas 4. Whisk the butter and sugar together until pale and fluffy, then beat in the marmalade and the eggs, one at a time.

Mix the instant coffee with the boiling water, then whisk it into the mixture. Gently fold in the self-raising flour and baking powder, taking care not to overmix. Spoon the batter into a lined 20cm x 26cm roasting tin.

Transfer the cake to the oven and bake for 25–30 minutes, until firm to the touch and a skewer inserted comes out clean.

While the cake is cooking, make the marmalade coffee syrup. Mix the instant coffee with the boiling water in a small saucepan, add the marmalade and stir over a low heat. Bring to the boil, simmer for 1 minute, then leave to cool.

Once the cake is cooked, leave it in the tin to cool for 5 minutes, then gently lift it out on to a wire rack. Use a skewer to make a few holes in the top, then pour over the syrup.

Serve warm or at room temperature. Any leftovers will keep well in an airtight tin in a cool room for 2–3 days.

FOR DIABETICS: replace the sugar with 60g xylitol, and use sugar-free marmalade.

ORANGE & HAZELNUT CAKE

A nice simple citrus-spiked cake, with ground hazelnuts in the sponge and a crunchy topping of toasted hazelnuts on top.

Serves: 8
Prep: 15 minutes
Cook: 30–35 minutes

175g softened unsalted butter
175g caster sugar
3 medium free-range eggs
1 large orange, zest and juice
50g ground hazelnuts
120g self-raising flour
1 teaspoon baking powder

TOPPING
100g icing sugar
20ml orange juice
50g toasted hazelnuts,
   chopped

Preheat the oven to 160°C fan/180°C/gas 4. Whisk the butter and sugar together until pale and fluffy, then beat in the eggs one at a time, along with the orange zest and juice.

Gently fold in the ground hazelnuts, self-raising flour and baking powder, taking care not to overmix. Spoon the batter into a lined 20cm x 26cm roasting tin.

Transfer the cake to the oven and bake for 30–35 minutes, until firm to the touch and a skewer inserted comes out clean.

Leave the cake in the tin for 5 minutes, then gently lift it out on to a wire rack and leave to cool completely.

For the icing, mix the icing sugar and orange juice together, then drizzle over the cake. Scatter with the chopped toasted hazelnuts and leave to set before serving.

Any leftovers will keep well in an airtight tin in a cool room for 2–3 days.

FOR GLUTEN-FREE: this works really well using Freee gluten-free self-raising flour from Doves Farm in place of the ordinary self-raising flour.

FOR DIABETICS: replace the sugar with 80g xylitol.

APPLE & PINE NUT CAKE

This cake has a wonderful texture and flavour from the pine nuts – a lovely cake to make in the autumn when you're looking for ways to use up a glut of apples. The cardamom gives a very light background flavour: I'd have this cake in the afternoon with a cup of coffee.

Serves: 8
Prep: 15 minutes
Cook: 35–40 minutes

100g pine nuts
170g softened unsalted butter
170g caster sugar
3 medium free-range eggs
125g self-raising flour
1 teaspoon baking powder
4 cardamom pods, seeds only
2 medium apples, chopped

Preheat the oven to 160°C fan/180°C/gas 4. Use a food processor or spice grinder to blitz 75g of the pine nuts until fairly finely ground – don't overblitz, or they'll release too much oil. Set aside.

Whisk the butter and sugar together until pale and fluffy, then beat in the eggs one at a time.

Gently fold in the self-raising flour, ground pine nuts, baking powder and cardamom seeds, taking care not to overmix. Spoon the batter into a lined 20cm x 26cm roasting tin.

Scatter the chopped apple and remaining whole pine nuts over the cake, then transfer to the oven and bake for 35–40 minutes, until firm to the touch and a skewer inserted comes out clean.

Leave the cake in the tin for 5 minutes, then gently lift it out on to a wire rack and leave to cool briefly before serving warm or at room temperature.

Any leftovers should be stored in the fridge: you can gently warm the slices in the microwave as needed.

FOR GLUTEN-FREE: replace the self-raising flour with gluten-free self-raising flour.

FOR DIABETICS: replace the sugar with 80g xylitol.

SPICED CARROT & COCONUT CAKE

This is my all-time favourite carrot cake: the coconut and gram flour add a wonderful texture and flavour, and incidentally, make the cake suitable for gluten-free baking. If you don't have gram flour to hand, you can substitute with ordinary plain or gluten-free plain flour.

Serves: 8
Prep: 15 minutes
Cook: 35–40 minutes

125ml olive oil
170g soft dark brown sugar
3 medium free-range eggs
400g grated carrot
170g gram flour
(or plain flour, if not making gluten-free)
65g desiccated coconut
1½ teaspoons baking powder
1 teaspoon ground cinnamon
½ teaspoon grated nutmeg

ICING
40g icing sugar
180g cream cheese
1 tablespoon lemon juice

Preheat the oven to 160°C fan/180°C/gas 4. Whisk the olive oil and sugar together, then beat in the eggs one by one.

In a separate bowl, stir the grated carrot, gram or plain flour, desiccated coconut, baking powder, cinnamon and nutmeg together, then add this to the liquid ingredients. Stir gently until combined.

Transfer the mix to a lined 20cm x 26cm roasting tin and bake for 35–40 minutes, until well risen and firm to the touch.

Let the cake cool for 10 minutes in the tin before removing to a wire rack to cool completely.

Beat the icing sugar, cream cheese and lemon juice together and spread evenly over the cake before serving (tiny edible carrots to decorate optional).

MUFFIN TINS

BLACKBERRY CREAM CHEESE

INTENSE CHOCOLATE SALTED CARAMEL

RASPBERRY, LEMON & HAZELNUT CRUMBLE

PEANUT BUTTER, RASPBERRY & BANANA
(VEGAN)

BLACK PEPPER, CHEDDAR & SAGE
(DIABETIC-FRIENDLY)

GOAT'S CHEESE, FIG & BASIL

ROASTED TOMATO, RICOTTA & THYME
(DIABETIC-FRIENDLY)

CHILLI -SPIKED HALLOUMI & COURGETTE
(DIABETIC-FRIENDLY)

MUFFIN TINS

Mini muffins, giant breakfast muffins, savoury canapé muffins – I love them all. And what I love best is that you can usually knock them out without very much more effort than a quick fridge, cupboard or freezer raid. The recipes in this chapter all rely largely on storecupboard ingredients – I inevitably use frozen and defrosted raspberries and blackberries, and if the urgent need to make muffins comes upon me and I've run out of milk or eggs, almost all the sweet muffin recipes can be easily adapted using bananas, peanut butter or a combination of the two.

I give you my customisable base recipe on the next page, with notes as follows:

FLOUR

I use self-raising as standard, but enjoy experimenting, particularly with savoury muffins – half rye and half self-raising, half spelt and half self-raising, sometimes a bit of buckwheat. Bear in mind that these flours may need a little extra 'oompf' to rise, which leads me to . . .

BAKING POWDER

Necessary for a good rise, but too much and you will have exploding muffins. One level ordinary teaspoon is fine – but add in an extra half-teaspoon if you're baking with plain or any of the more interesting flours. Use 2 teaspoons for vegan muffins, because you don't have the egg to provide extra lift.

SUGAR

I like to use soft light brown sugar in muffins (or soft dark brown sugar) – it gives a fudgier texture and taste. Look out for unrefined sugar for the best flavour, as some larger brands just use ordinary caster sugar and smush it up with extracted molasses for colour rather than selling you the real stuff. If it doesn't say 'unrefined' on the label, it's not – I buy Billingtons.

If you're baking for a diabetic, use the same quantity of date syrup for a similarly treacly flavour.

OIL VS BUTTER

After some experimentation I've come to the conclusion that olive oil works much better than butter in muffins – no idea why. Save the butter for your crumble toppings, and use olive or any other neutral oil for the best texture.

LIQUIDS

A mixture of yogurt and milk adds lightness, and you could replace this with all buttermilk, or experiment with cream cheese, as in the blackberry cream cheese muffins on page 38.

Eggs: just one medium free-range egg is fine to get a good lift.

If you're making vegan muffins, use mashed ripe bananas, peanut butter or a mixture of both: it serves the function of the liquid and the eggs. Three mashed bananas are a good replacement for the yogurt, milk and eggs in any of the sweet recipes, but reduce the amount of sugar, as the banana provides more than enough. You could certainly experiment with almond, hazelnut or pumpkin seed butter too, using the weight in the original recipe as a guide.

ALL-PURPOSE SWEET MUFFIN

250g self-raising flour

1 level teaspoon baking powder

150g soft light brown sugar

100ml olive oil

150g natural yogurt

100ml milk

1 medium free-range egg,
lightly beaten

VEGAN SWEET MUFFIN

250g self-raising flour

2 level teaspoons baking powder

80g soft light brown sugar

3 bananas, mashed

50g crunchy peanut butter

100ml olive oil

30ml water

SAVOURY MUFFIN

250g self-raising flour

+ grated cheese of your choice

1 level teaspoon baking powder

1 teaspoon sea salt flakes

100ml olive oil

150g natural yogurt

50ml milk

1 medium free range egg,
lightly beaten

BLACKBERRY CREAM CHEESE MUFFINS

These are nice, easy breakfast muffins – I prefer blackberries to blueberries (though by all means use the latter if you like). Using cream cheese in the mixture gives a lovely texture to the finished muffins – serve them with more cream cheese alongside, if you wish.

Makes: 12–14 muffins
Prep: 15 minutes
Cook: 20–25 minutes

250g self-raising flour
1 level teaspoon baking powder
150g soft light brown sugar
100ml olive oil
150g cream cheese
100ml milk
1 medium free-range egg,
   lightly beaten
200g blackberries,
   halved if large

TOPPING
2 tablespoons demerara sugar

Preheat the oven to 180°C fan/200°C/gas 6. Stir the self-raising flour, baking powder and sugar together in a large bowl.

In a separate bowl or a large jug, beat the olive oil, cream cheese, milk and egg together. (This will be easier if you beat the cream cheese before adding the other ingredients.)

Very briefly stir the liquid into the flour and sugar mixture along with the blackberries until you can't see any flour, and no further – the less you mix, the lighter the muffin.

Divide your batter equally between 12 lined muffin cups (14 if your muffin cups are on the smaller side), then evenly scatter over the demerara sugar.

Transfer the muffins to the oven and bake for 20–25 minutes, until well risen and firm to the touch. Cool briefly on a wire rack and eat warm.

These are best eaten on the day they're made, as the crunchy topping won't survive overnight – but you can keep them in the fridge in an airtight container for up to 2 days, and reheat them gently in the oven as needed.

TO VEGANISE: replace the dairy and egg with 3 mashed bananas and 25ml oat milk. Reduce the sugar to 80g, and add another teaspoon of baking powder.

FOR DIABETICS: replace the sugar with 150ml date syrup, and omit the topping. Use flaked almonds instead for crunch.

INTENSE CHOCOLATE SALTED CARAMEL MUFFINS

I've been in search of the perfect chocolate muffin for years at bakery counters and coffee shops, and as the Platonic ideal kept eluding me, I decided to make my own. It may sound like an exaggeration, but these are hands down the best chocolate muffins I've had – and with an added surprise caramel hit on the inside.

Makes:	12 muffins
Prep:	15 minutes
Cook:	20 minutes

200g self-raising flour
50g cocoa powder
1 level teaspoon baking powder
Sea salt flakes
150g soft dark brown sugar
100ml olive oil
100g natural yogurt
150ml milk
1 medium free-range egg,
   lightly beaten
100g dark chocolate chips
   or chopped dark chocolate
   (ideally 70% cocoa solids)
12 round teaspoons
   dulce de leche
   or tinned caramel

Preheat the oven to 180°C fan/200°C/gas 6. Stir the self-raising flour, cocoa powder, baking powder and ½ teaspoon of sea salt together in a large bowl, then mix in the sugar.

In a separate bowl or a large jug, whisk the olive oil, yogurt, milk and egg together. Briefly stir the liquid into the flour and sugar mixture along with 75g of the chocolate chips, bearing in mind Nigella's advice that a lumpy batter makes the lightest muffin.

Spoon a tablespoon of muffin mixture into each of your 12 lined muffin cups, then add a teaspoon of dulce de leche to each. Add a pinch of sea salt, then spoon the remaining batter evenly into each cup to cover the caramel.

Scatter the rest of the chocolate chips over the muffins, then transfer to the oven and bake for 20 minutes, until well risen and firm to the touch.

Cool briefly on a wire rack and eat warm, or allow to cool completely and store in an airtight container in a cool room for up to a week.

TO VEGANISE: replace the dairy and egg with 3 mashed bananas and 25ml oat milk. Reduce the sugar to 80g, and add another teaspoon of baking powder. Replace the dulce de leche with date syrup, and use vegan chocolate.

FOR DIABETICS: replace the sugar with 150ml date syrup and add to the liquid ingredients. Replace the dulce de leche with date syrup and use diabetic-friendly dark chocolate

RASPBERRY, LEMON & HAZELNUT CRUMBLE MUFFINS

The hazelnut crumble topping for these muffins is so addictive that you'll be tempted to add it on top of all the other muffins too – and a good number of cakes. I can't claim that these are terribly healthy, but they are a lovely treat – perfect for a mid-afternoon pick-me-up with a cup of coffee.

Makes: 12 muffins
Prep: 15 minutes
Cook: 25–30 minutes

250g self-raising flour
1 level teaspoon baking powder
150g soft light brown sugar
    (or caster sugar)
1 lemon, zest only
100ml olive oil
200g natural yogurt
30ml lemon juice
1 medium free-range egg,
    lightly beaten
200g fresh or frozen
    and defrosted raspberries

CRUMBLE MIX
25g cubed unsalted butter
50g plain flour
50g hazelnuts, chopped
25g soft light brown sugar
A pinch of sea salt flakes

Preheat the oven to 180°C fan/200°C/gas 6. Stir the self-raising flour, baking powder, sugar and lemon zest together in a large bowl.

In a separate bowl or a large jug, whisk the olive oil, yogurt, lemon juice and egg together.

For the crumble mixture, use your fingertips to rub the butter, plain flour, hazelnuts, sugar and salt together into a rubbly granola-type mix. Set aside.

Very briefly stir the liquid ingredients into the flour, sugar and lemon zest mixture, along with the raspberries, just until you can't see any flour and no further – the less you mix, the lighter the muffin.

Divide your batter equally between 12 lined muffin cups, then evenly scatter over the crumble mixture.

Transfer the muffins to the oven and bake for 25–30 minutes, until well risen and firm to the touch. Cool briefly on a wire rack and eat warm.

These can be kept in the fridge in an airtight container for 2 days and reheated gently in the oven as needed.

PEANUT BUTTER, RASPBERRY & BANANA MUFFINS

Or, peanut butter and jelly muffins. While I'm not sure I actually ate anything with peanut butter and jelly as a child on holiday in the USA, I love the idea of it now – and it makes a change from piling sandwiches with peanut butter, bananas and chocolate. Though you could equally replace the raspberry jam in this with a spoon of Nutella…

Makes: 12 muffins
Prep: 15 minutes
Cook: 25 minutes

250g self-raising flour
2 level teaspoons baking powder
80g soft light brown sugar
3 bananas
  (approx. 400g skin on),
  mashed
50g crunchy peanut butter
100ml olive oil
30ml water
12 heaped teaspoons
  raspberry jam
24 fresh or frozen and
  defrosted raspberries
30g salted peanuts,
  roughly chopped

Preheat the oven to 180°C fan/200°C/gas 6. Stir the self-raising flour, baking powder and sugar together in a large bowl.

In a separate bowl or a large jug, beat the mashed bananas, peanut butter and olive oil together with the water.

Very briefly stir the banana mixture into the flour and sugar mixture just until you can't see the flour – the less you mix, the lighter the muffin.

Spoon a tablespoon of muffin mixture into each of your 12 lined muffin cups, then add a teaspoon of raspberry jam in the centre of each, along with 1 whole raspberry. Spoon the remaining batter evenly into each cup to cover the raspberries.

Scatter the chopped peanuts over the muffins, add a raspberry on top of each one, then transfer to the oven and bake for 25 minutes, until well risen and firm to the touch.

Cool briefly on a wire rack and serve warm. These are best eaten straight away, but you can keep them in an airtight container in a cool room for up to 3 days.

BLACK PEPPER, CHEDDAR & SAGE MUFFINS

I couldn't have a chapter on muffins without including savoury options, which between us are my favourite sort of muffin – as good for breakfast as they are for an afternoon snack. You could definitely think about making tiny versions of these in mini-muffin cups to hand around with pre-dinner drinks too – in which case they'll take no longer than 15 minutes in the oven.

Makes:	12 ordinary
	or 24 mini muffins
Prep:	15 minutes
Cook:	20–25 minutes

250g self-raising flour
35g strong cheddar cheese, grated
1 level teaspoon baking powder
1 teaspoon sea salt flakes
1 tablespoon freshly ground black pepper
20 sage leaves, roughly chopped
100ml olive oil
150g natural yogurt
50ml milk
1 medium free-range egg, lightly beaten

TOPPING
50g cheddar cheese, grated
12 sage leaves
Freshly ground black pepper

Preheat the oven to 180°C fan/200°C/gas 6. Stir the self-raising flour, cheddar cheese, baking powder, sea salt, pepper and chopped sage together in a large bowl.

In a separate bowl or a large jug, whisk the olive oil, yogurt, milk and egg together. Very briefly stir the liquid into the flour and cheese mixture just until you can't see any flour, and no further – the less you mix, the lighter the muffin.

Divide the muffin mixture between 12 lined muffin cups, then evenly scatter over the cheddar cheese and sage leaves for the topping, with a small grind of black pepper.

Transfer the muffins to the oven and bake for 20–25 minutes, until well risen and firm to the touch. Cool briefly on a wire rack and eat warm. These are best eaten on the day they're made, but they can be kept in the fridge in an airtight container for 2 days and reheated gently in the oven as needed.

FOR GLUTEN-FREE: replace the self-raising flour with a good brand of gluten-free flour, or a mixture of gluten-free and buckwheat.

GOAT'S CHEESE, FIG & BASIL MUFFINS

This is a muffin version of my favourite canapé – introduced to me by my friend Charlotte at university, and rolled out at pretty much every party I've ever given since. The combination of goat's cheese, fig and pesto with a squeeze of honey is just perfect – in the absence of small rounds of baguette for crostini, this makes an excellent alternative. You could also make these with feta instead of goat's cheese.

Makes: 12 ordinary or 24 mini muffins
Prep: 20 minutes
Cook: 20–25 minutes

250g self-raising flour
100g strong goat's cheese, chopped
1 level teaspoon baking powder
1 teaspoon sea salt flakes
Freshly ground black pepper
100ml olive oil
150g natural yogurt
50g chilled fresh basil pesto
1 medium free-range egg, lightly beaten

TOPPING
50g strong goat's cheese, finely sliced
12 slices of fresh fig

TO SERVE
Honey, to squeeze
Fresh rosemary (optional)

Preheat the oven to 180°C fan/200°C/gas 6. Stir the self-raising flour, goat's cheese, baking powder, sea salt and a good grind of black pepper together in a large bowl.

In a separate bowl or a large jug, whisk the olive oil, yogurt, pesto and egg together. Very briefly stir the liquid into the flour and cheese, just until you can't see any flour and no further – the less you mix, the lighter the muffin.

Divide your mixture evenly between 12 lined muffin cups, then scatter over the sliced goat's cheese. Top each muffin with a slice of fig, then transfer the muffins to the oven and bake for 20–25 minutes.

Once the muffins are well risen and firm to the touch, cool briefly on a wire rack and serve warm, with a squeeze of honey and scattered with the fresh rosemary, if using.

These are best eaten on the day they're made, but they can be kept in the fridge in an airtight container for 2 days and reheated gently in the oven as needed.

FOR DIABETICS: omit the honey at the end.

FOR GLUTEN-FREE: replace the self-raising flour with a good brand of gluten-free flour, or a mixture of gluten-free self-raising flour and buckwheat.

ROASTED TOMATO, RICOTTA & THYME MUFFINS

These muffins require slightly more effort, in that you roast a tray of cherry tomatoes to intensify the flavour before stirring them into the muffin batter, but it's well worth the pay-off – they work beautifully with the ricotta and thyme. I like to use rye flour in these muffins for the depth of flavour, but if you only have self-raising that's fine, just use 250g as in the other recipes, and reduce the amount of baking powder to 1 level teaspoon.

Makes: 12 muffins
Prep: 15 minutes
Cook: 50–55 minutes

TOMATOES
125g cherry tomatoes,
    halved, and the vines
1 tablespoon olive oil
Sea salt and freshly ground
    black pepper

MUFFINS
125g self-raising flour
125g rye flour
1½ teaspoons baking powder
1 teaspoon sea salt flakes
A small bundle of thyme leaves
100ml olive oil
150g natural yogurt
50ml milk
100g ricotta
1 medium free-range egg,
    lightly beaten

FOR GLUTEN-FREE: replace the flours with a good brand of gluten-free flour, or a mixture of gluten-free and buckwheat.

Preheat the oven to 160°C fan/180°C/gas 4. Tip the cherry tomatoes and their vines into a small lined roasting tin, arrange cut-side up, then drizzle over a tablespoon of olive oil and season with a little salt and pepper. Roast for 30 minutes, then leave to cool for 10.

Meanwhile, stir the flours, baking powder and sea salt together in a large bowl with about a teaspoon of the thyme leaves.

In a separate bowl, beat the olive oil, yogurt, milk, half the ricotta and the egg together, and set aside.

Stir half the tomatoes into the ricotta and egg mix with the flours, mixing very briefly just until you can't see the flour – the less you mix, the lighter the muffin.

Divide the muffin mixture between your 12 lined muffin cups and top with a teaspoon of the remaining ricotta. Evenly scatter the rest of the roasted cherry tomatoes and thyme leaves over the muffins.

Transfer the tin to the oven and bake for 20–25 minutes, until the muffins are well risen and firm to the touch.

Cool briefly on a wire rack and eat warm. These are best eaten on the day they're made, but can be kept in the fridge in an airtight container for 2 days and reheated gently in the oven as needed.

CHILLI-SPIKED HALLOUMI & COURGETTE MUFFINS

These muffins are inspired by my all-time favourite savoury muffin from Laura Goodman's cookbook *Carbs* – here I've adapted them into my muffin 'formula' with chilli for a bit of a kick. They'd go really well alongside soup for lunch, or, as with all the savoury muffins, made into a mini-version for canapés.

Makes:	12 ordinary or 24 mini muffins
Prep:	15 minutes
Cook:	20–25 minutes

2 courgettes (approx. 400g), grated
2 teaspoons sea salt flakes
250g self-raising flour
1 level teaspoon baking powder
125g halloumi, grated
1–2 teaspoons chipotle chilli flakes
100ml olive oil
50g natural yogurt
1 medium free-range egg, lightly beaten
3 spring onions, finely sliced

TOPPING
50g halloumi, cut into little cubes
1 red chilli, finely sliced

Preheat the oven to 180°C fan/200°C/gas 6. Tip the grated courgette into a large bowl with a teaspoon of the sea salt, and mix. Leave to sit for 5 minutes, then wrap in a tea towel or a clean J-cloth and squeeze out as much liquid as you can – this will radically improve the texture of the muffins, so don't be tempted to skip it.

Stir the self-raising flour, baking powder, grated halloumi, remaining sea salt and chilli flakes together in a large bowl.

In a separate bowl or a large jug, whisk the olive oil, yogurt and egg together with the grated courgettes and the spring onions. Very briefly stir the courgette and egg mixture into the flour and cheese, just until you can't see any flour and no further – the less you mix, the lighter the muffin.

Divide the muffin mixture between your 12 lined muffin cups, then evenly scatter over the halloumi cubes and some sliced chilli.

Transfer the muffins to the oven and bake for 20–25 minutes, until well risen and firm to the touch. Cool briefly on a wire rack and eat warm. These are best eaten on the day they're made, but they can be kept in the fridge in an airtight container for 2 days and reheated gently in the oven as needed.

FOR GLUTEN-FREE: replace the self-raising flour with a good brand of gluten-free flour, or a mixture of gluten-free and buckwheat.

NOTE: for canapé-size versions, use a lined mini-muffin tin and bake for 12–15 minutes, until cooked through.

LOAF TINS

VANILLA & BAY

STICKY DATE GINGERBREAD
(DIABETIC-FRIENDLY)

CHOCOLATE & ROSEMARY

SAFFRON & ORANGE BANANA BREAD
(VEGAN)

MARZIPAN, LEMON & CARDAMOM

AFTERNOON TEA LOAF

LOAF TINS

Loaf cakes are so pleasing – simple and unfussy. I find them rather reassuring to have stashed in a tin for cake emergencies – and unlike other shapes of cake, I think they lend themselves particularly well to breakfast time. Chocolate loaf cakes are among my favourite things, particularly spiked with large chunks of chocolate, as with the chocolate and rosemary loaf on page 64, but simpler variations like the vanilla and bay on page 60 will fill your house with the most incredible scent, and really can't be beaten with a cup of tea. There is incidentally half a vanilla and bay loaf sitting invitingly in the tin next door as I write, and I'm tempted to cut a thick slice at the risk of spoiling my appetite for lunch. Of course, if you're in a hurry or have a penchant for interestingly shaped cake tins, the marzipan and lemon loaves on page 68 are rather lovely made in individual loaf tins – and take much less time to cook. (An update: I did sneak a pre-lunch slice of cake.)

You'll notice in my classic loaf formula overleaf that unlike the 6-6-6 formula of the traybake cakes chapter, there's a slightly increased proportion of self-raising flour to the other ingredients. I tend not to add extra baking powder, as 8 ounces (or 230g) of self-raising flour seems to have enough already. If you are using nut flours it is worth adding a scant teaspoon extra.

Troubleshooting: the last thing you want is a loaf with a sunken middle – it'll taste fine, but aesthetically, it's a bit meh. So bear in mind: sunken cakes are usually a result of too much raising agent (hence no added baking powder), a too-hot oven, or taking it out too early and having to keep putting it back in for longer. A nice long stint for 50 minutes – no opening the oven door – and you're golden.

BASIC LOAF

170g softened unsalted butter

170g caster sugar
(golden if preferred)

3 medium free-range eggs

230g self-raising flour

FOR DIABETIC-FRIENDLY LOAF CAKES

swap out the
170g caster sugar
for 85g xylitol,
or 170ml date syrup

BASIC VEGAN LOAF

170g olive or coconut oil

130g soft light brown sugar

4 ripe medium bananas
(approx. 300g), mashed

230g self-raising flour

BASIC GLUTEN-FREE LOAF

170g softened unsalted butter

170g caster sugar
(golden if preferred)

3 medium free-range eggs

100g ground almonds
/hazelnuts/pistachios

130g gluten-free
self-raising flour

ADDITIONAL FLAVOURINGS

vanilla

lemon/orange/lime
zest and juice

cinnamon

ginger

dried fruit

swapping out the
caster sugar
for soft light brown etc.

VANILLA & BAY LOAF

This is a lovely, subtle loaf, with the bay adding a herbaceous note alongside the classic vanilla. If you have time, you can steep the bay for longer than the time it takes to make the cake batter – it'll give you a more pronounced flavour. One to make when you're in the mood for a proper slice of cake.

Serves: 8
Prep: 15 minutes
Cook: 45–50 minutes

40ml milk
3 bay leaves
170g softened unsalted butter
170g caster sugar
   (golden if preferred)
1 heaped teaspoon vanilla extract
   (or seeds scraped from
   ½ vanilla pod)
3 medium free-range eggs
230g self-raising flour
1 teaspoon baking powder

Preheat the oven to 160°C fan/180°C/gas 4. Heat the milk in a small saucepan with the bay leaves; when it comes to the boil, immediately turn off the heat and leave to steep.

Whisk the butter and sugar together with the vanilla extract or seeds until pale and fluffy, then beat in the eggs one at a time.

Gently fold in the self-raising flour and baking powder, taking care not to overmix, then stir in the infused milk, reserving the bay leaves. Spoon the batter into a lined 900g loaf tin.

Lay the bay leaves over the top of the cake, then transfer to the oven and bake for 45–50 minutes, until firm to the touch and a skewer inserted comes out clean.

Leave the cake in the tin for 5 minutes, then gently lift it out on to a wire rack and leave to cool briefly before serving warm or at room temperature.

The cake will keep well in an airtight container in a cool room for 2–3 days.

FOR GLUTEN-FREE: replace the self-raising flour with a good brand of gluten-free self-raising flour (I like Freee, from Doves Farm), or a 50:50 mix of ground almonds and gluten-free self-raising flour.

FOR DIABETICS: replace the caster sugar with 80g xylitol.

STICKY DATE GINGERBREAD

This was one of the first cakes I made for this book: a wonderfully sticky, rich loaf cake. You can substitute soft dark brown sugar for the date syrup if you wish, but the date syrup gives a wonderfully intense depth of flavour to the cake, and incidentally makes it suitable for diabetics.

Serves: 8
Prep: 15 minutes
Cook: 40–45 minutes

170ml olive oil
170ml date syrup
3 medium free-range eggs
230g self-raising flour
1 teaspoon baking powder
2 heaped teaspoons
  ground ginger
175g Medjool dates,
  torn or chopped

Preheat the oven to 160°C fan/180°C/gas 4. Whisk the olive oil and date syrup together, and when smoothly incorporated, beat in the eggs one at a time.

Gently fold in the self-raising flour, baking powder and ground ginger, taking care not to overmix.

Spoon two-thirds of the batter into a lined 900g loaf tin, and scatter over the torn or chopped Medjool dates. Cover with the remaining third of the batter.

Transfer the tin to the oven and bake for 40–45 minutes, until firm to the touch and a skewer inserted comes out clean.

Let the cake cool on a wire rack: I feel it needs no adornment, but you could make a simple glacé icing using the recipe on page 26 to drizzle over if you like.

Serve warm or at room temperature: the cake will keep well in an airtight container in a cool room for 2–3 days.

CHOCOLATE & ROSEMARY LOAF

Chocolate loaf cakes are among my favourite – possibly as I over-indulged on Mr Kipling's very chocolatey mini loaf cakes as a child, with their chocolate chips and thick layer of chocolate fondant icing. This triple chocolate version – including the all-important chips – includes rosemary for a subtle herbal note, and a thick ganache topping, with a yogurt base for a beautifully textured sponge.

Serves: 8
Prep: 15 minutes
Cook: 45–50 minutes

120g natural full-fat yogurt
50ml olive oil
170g soft dark brown sugar
3 medium free-range eggs
120g self-raising flour
1 teaspoon baking powder
50g cocoa powder
2 sprigs of rosemary,
    needles finely chopped
30ml milk
100g dark chocolate
    (70% cocoa solids),
    cut into small chunks

GANACHE
100ml double cream
2 large sprigs of rosemary
100g dark chocolate,
    finely chopped or blitzed

FOR DIABETICS: replace the dark brown sugar with 170ml date syrup and use diabetic-friendly dark chocolate.

Preheat the oven to 160°C fan/180°C/gas 4. Whisk the yogurt, olive oil and sugar together; when smoothly incorporated, beat in the eggs one at a time.

Gently fold in the self-raising flour, baking powder, cocoa powder and rosemary, taking care not to overmix. Stir in the milk, then transfer the mix to a lined 900g loaf tin.

Scatter the chocolate chunks all over the cake mix, and use a teaspoon to gently stir them into the top layer of the cake. (They will try to sink, so don't stir vigorously, this is more to half-cover them with a thin layer of cake batter.)

Transfer to the oven and bake for 45–50 minutes, until firm to the touch and a skewer inserted comes out clean (less any chocolate chips that you hit).

Let the cake cool on a wire rack. Once cool to the touch, you can start on the ganache: heat the double cream in a saucepan until just under boiling, along with 1 sprig of rosemary. Tip the finely chopped or blitzed dark chocolate into a large bowl and pour the hot cream over the top, removing the rosemary. Let it sit for 2 minutes, then whisk quickly until smooth and glossy.

Spread the ganache over the cake and place the remaining rosemary sprig on top. Serve once the ganache has set: the cake will keep well in an airtight container in a cool room for 2–3 days.

SAFFRON & ORANGE BANANA BREAD

My favourite types of banana bread are vegan – I find you don't need eggs for a wonderful flavour and texture. Use the best saffron you can find, as a little goes a long way – Belazu is an excellent and easily available brand, found in larger supermarkets.

Serves: 6
Prep: 15 minutes
Cook: 45–50 minutes

A large pinch of good saffron
   threads
2 tablespoons boiling water
170ml olive oil
130g soft light brown sugar
1 orange, zest and juice
4 ripe medium bananas
   (approx. 300g), mashed
250g self-raising flour
1 teaspoon baking powder
50g pine nuts

Preheat the oven to 160°C fan/180°C/gas 4. Put the saffron threads into a mug with the boiling water and leave to steep for 5 minutes, then use the back of a spoon to mash the saffron against the side of the mug to release the colour.

Whisk the olive oil, sugar, orange zest and juice and the mashed bananas together with the saffron and water, then gently fold in the self-raising flour and baking powder.

Spoon the batter into a lined 900g loaf tin and scatter the pine nuts evenly over the top. Transfer the tin to the oven and bake for 45–50 minutes, until well risen, firm to the touch and a skewer inserted comes out clean.

Let the cake cool briefly on a wire rack and serve warm or at room temperature: the cake will keep well in an airtight container in a cool room for 2–3 days.

NOTE: if you know your oven runs hot, cover the loaf tin with tinfoil after 30 minutes to prevent the pine nuts browning too much.

MARZIPAN, LEMON & CARDAMOM LOAF

Many of my favourite things in one loaf: this chapter wouldn't be complete without a lemon cake, and as for some reason I've never got on with lemon drizzle, this cake is spiked with golden pieces of marzipan instead. Extremely moreish – especially baked in mini-loaf tins.

Serves: 8
Prep: 15 minutes
Cook: 45–50 minutes
(or 25 minutes
in mini-loaf tins)

170g softened unsalted butter
170g caster sugar
(golden if preferred)
3 medium free-range eggs
1 lemon, zest and juice
230g self-raising flour
1 teaspoon baking powder
4 cardamom pods,
seeds ground,
outer pods discarded
100g marzipan,
chopped into 1cm chunks

Preheat the oven to 160°C fan/180°C/gas 4. Whisk the butter and sugar together until pale and fluffy, then beat in the eggs one at a time, followed by the lemon zest and juice.

Gently fold in the self-raising flour, baking powder and ground cardamom, taking care not to overmix. Transfer the batter to a lined 900g loaf or between 8 mini-loaf tins.

Scatter the marzipan chunks all over the cake mix, then transfer to the oven and bake for 45–50 minutes for a large loaf or 25 minutes for mini loaves, until firm to the touch and a skewer inserted comes out clean (less any bits of marzipan that you hit).

Let the cake cool briefly on a wire rack before slicing and serving warm.

The cake will keep well in an airtight container in a cool room for 2–3 days.

FOR GLUTEN-FREE: replace the self-raising flour with a 50:50 mix of ground almonds and gluten-free self-raising flour.

AFTERNOON TEA LOAF

This recipe comes from one of my parents' first friends and neighbours when they moved to England. Denise Palmer taught my mother how to make a Victoria sponge, scones and this absolutely wonderful lightly fruited cake. She called it a 'boiled cake', as you melt the butter, sugar and fruit together before stirring in the eggs and flour. I've updated the recipe slightly to a tea loaf – a wonderfully comforting classic.

Serves: 8
Prep: 15 minutes
Cook: 40–45 minutes

250ml boiling water
2 English Breakfast teabags
115g unsalted butter
115g soft dark brown sugar
170g mixed raisins and sultanas
2 medium free-range eggs
200g self-raising flour
1 teaspoon mixed spice,
    allspice or cinnamon
A pinch of sea salt

Preheat the oven to 160°C fan/180°C/gas 4. Tip the boiling water into a saucepan and add the teabags. Leave them to steep for 4 minutes, then remove and discard.

Add the butter, sugar, raisins and sultanas to the pan and bring to the boil. Lower the heat and simmer for 2 minutes, then turn off the heat and leave to cool.

Once the mixture has cooled, beat in the eggs, one at a time.

Weigh out the self-raising flour and spice of your choice into a large bowl, add the salt, then pour in the liquid ingredients and gently stir until just incorporated. Spoon the batter into a lined 900g loaf tin, then transfer to the oven and bake for 40–45 minutes, until firm to the touch and a skewer inserted comes out clean.

Leave the cake in the tin for 5 minutes, then gently lift it out on to a wire rack and leave to cool briefly before serving warm or at room temperature.

The cake will keep well in an airtight container in a cool room for 2–3 days.

FOR DIABETICS: replace the soft dark brown sugar with 115ml date syrup.

FOR GLUTEN-FREE: replace the self-raising flour with a good brand of gluten-free self-raising flour or a 50:50 mix of ground almonds and gluten-free self-raising flour.

BROWNIES

CHOCOLATE PASSIONFRUIT

(GLUTEN-FREE)

CARAMEL PECAN

(GLUTEN-FREE)

STEM-GINGER, CHERRY & ALMOND

(GLUTEN-FREE)

RHUBARB & CUSTARD BLONDIES

PISTACHIO & DATE

(GLUTEN-FREE, DIABETIC-FRIENDLY)

BAKED MASCARPONE, CHERRY & WALNUT

(GLUTEN-FREE)

BROWNIES

The search for the perfect brownie has at times felt like a lifelong pursuit: and it is now one that I've happily concluded – particularly after making the stem ginger, cherry and almond version on page 82. Just thinking about them makes me want to head into the kitchen and start studding melted chocolate with translucent shards of crystallised ginger and sticky glacé cherries, then sit in front of the oven for all of fifteen minutes before diving in with a spoon. Words fail – you will have to try it yourself.

I've combined chocolate with some of my favourite ingredients in this chapter – passionfruit, caramel, salt, pecans, pistachios – and, for the wildcard blondie recipe, with rhubarb and vanilla custard. The baked mascarpone and cherry brownies on page 88 are more pudding-like, while you could wheel out the pistachio and date brownies at any time, from a mid-morning coffee to tiny petit-four squares after dinner.

Apart from the blondies the recipes are all naturally gluten-free, as I realised during testing that for the squashiest brownie, flour is really an unnecessary ingredient – all the brownie recipes in this chapter use ground almonds (apart from the pistachio brownies, which suggest ground pistachios). I highly recommend that you ditch the flour too, unless you have a nut allergy, in which case use plain flour.

BASIC BROWNIE

85ml olive oil

90g soft dark brown sugar

50g dark chocolate (70% cocoa solids), chopped

70ml milk

2 medium free-range eggs

40g cocoa powder

60g ground almonds

A pinch of sea salt flakes

DIABETIC-FRIENDLY BROWNIE

85ml olive oil

125ml date syrup

50g diabetic-friendly dark chocolate (70% cocoa solids)

70ml milk

2 medium free-range eggs

40g cocoa powder

60g ground almonds

A pinch of sea salt flakes

ADDITIONAL FLAVOURINGS

raspberries

figs

macadamias

walnuts

cherries
(sour, sweet, fresh or frozen)

mango (for blondies)

CHOCOLATE PASSIONFRUIT BROWNIES

Chocolate and passionfruit are one of my favourite combinations and they work beautifully together here, with the bright acidity of the passionfruit providing a contrast to the rich, truffle-like brownie. An excellent pudding.

Serves: 8
Prep: 15 minutes
Cook: 12–15 minutes

85ml olive oil
90g soft dark brown sugar
50g dark chocolate
    (70% cocoa solids), chopped
70ml milk
2 medium free-range eggs
40g cocoa powder
60g ground almonds
A pinch of sea salt flakes
4 passionfruit, pulp only

Preheat the oven to 160°C fan/180°C/gas 4. Measure the olive oil, sugar and chocolate into a saucepan, then stir over a low heat until the chocolate has melted and the mixture is glossy.

Stir in the milk, then let the mixture cool for 5–10 minutes before whisking in the eggs.

Stir the cocoa powder, ground almonds and sea salt into the liquid mixture.

Pour the batter into a lined 24.5cm x 17.5cm baking tin and drop in tablespoons of the passionfruit pulp. Use the handle of a teaspoon to draw the passionfruit gently through the chocolate mixture.

Transfer the tin to the oven and bake for 12–15 minutes, until the top of the brownie looks just set. Let the brownie cool in the tin for 5 minutes before transferring it gently to a wire rack.

Serve warm or at room temperature. Store any leftovers in the fridge.

FOR DIABETICS: replace the sugar with 125ml date syrup, and use diabetic-friendly dark chocolate.

CARAMEL PECAN BROWNIES

This brownie is inspired by the American chocolates known as Turtles – a combination of caramel, pecans and chocolate. I love swirling the caramel through the chocolate mixture right at the end as a textural contrast: perfect served warm as a dessert, with ice cream alongside.

Serves: 8
Prep: 15 minutes
Cook: 12–15 minutes

85ml olive oil
90g soft dark brown sugar
50g dark chocolate
(70% cocoa solids), chopped
70ml milk
2 medium free-range eggs
40g cocoa powder
60g ground almonds
1 teaspoon sea salt flakes
100g pecans, roughly broken
75g tinned caramel
or dulce de leche, beaten

Preheat the oven to 160°C fan/180°C/gas 4. Measure the olive oil, sugar and chocolate into a saucepan, then stir over a low heat until the chocolate has melted and the mixture is glossy.

Stir in the milk, then let the mixture cool for 5–10 minutes before whisking in the eggs.

Stir the cocoa powder, ground almonds, ½ teaspoon of sea salt flakes and 50g of the broken pecans into the liquid mixture.

Pour the batter into a lined 24.5cm x 17.5cm baking tin and drop in tablespoons of the caramel or dulce de leche. Use the handle of a teaspoon to draw the caramel gently through the chocolate mixture, then scatter over the remaining pecans and sea salt.

Transfer the tin to the oven and bake for 12–15 minutes, until the top of the brownie looks just set. Let the brownie cool in the tin for 5 minutes before transferring it gently to a wire rack.

Serve warm or at room temperature. This will keep well in an airtight container for 2–3 days.

STEM GINGER, CHERRY & ALMOND BROWNIES

These are inspired by Florentine biscuits with their beautiful random mosaic of glacé cherries, almonds and candied fruit. I like crystallised ginger best of all candied fruit, but you could certainly add angelica or similar if you have any about. Addictive.

Serves:	8
Prep:	15 minutes
Cook:	12–15 minutes

85ml olive oil
90g soft dark brown sugar
50g dark chocolate
   (70% cocoa solids), chopped
70ml milk
2 medium free-range eggs
40g cocoa powder
60g ground almonds
A pinch of sea salt flakes
100g crystallised stem ginger,
   chopped
100g glacé cherries, chopped
100g blanched almonds,
   roughly chopped

Preheat the oven to 160°C fan/180°C/gas 4. Measure the olive oil, sugar and chocolate into a saucepan, then stir over a low heat until the chocolate has melted and the mixture is glossy.

Stir in the milk, then let the mixture cool for 5–10 minutes before whisking in the eggs.

Stir the cocoa powder, ground almonds, sea salt and 60g each of the ginger, cherries and almonds into the liquid mixture.

Pour the batter into a lined 24.5cm x 17.5cm baking tin, and scatter over the remaining 40g each of the ginger, cherries and almonds – I do these one at a time for a nice random pattern, as opposite.

Transfer the tin to the oven and bake for 12–15 minutes, until the top of the brownie looks just set. Let the brownie cool in the tin for 5 minutes before transferring it gently to a wire rack.

Serve warm or at room temperature. This will keep well in an airtight container for 2–3 days.

RHUBARB & CUSTARD BLONDIES

The sharpness of the roasted rhubarb provides an incredible contrast to the sweetness of the custard in these mildly addictive blondies. To save time, I suggest making a condensed milk custard, but if you wish to reduce the sugar, by all means use 100ml of home-made or shop-bought custard instead.

Serves: 8
Prep: 20 minutes
Cook: 40 minutes

400g rhubarb (ideally bright pink)
60g caster sugar
85ml olive oil
80g soft dark brown sugar
2 medium free-range egg whites
   (keep the yolks for the custard
   below)
1 medium free-range egg
150g plain flour
A pinch of sea salt flakes
70ml milk
A handful of hazelnuts,
   roughly chopped

CUSTARD
2 medium free-range egg yolks
   (left over from the egg
   whites above)
100g condensed milk

Preheat the oven to 170°C fan/190°C/gas 5. Cut the rhubarb into 2.5cm pieces, then mix with the caster sugar in a medium roasting tin. Transfer to the oven and roast for 20 minutes.

Once the rhubarb is cooked, lower the oven temperature to 160°C fan/180°C/gas 4.

Whisk the olive oil and soft brown sugar together with the egg whites and the whole egg until smoothly incorporated. Stir in the plain flour, salt and milk, then transfer the batter to a lined 24.5cm x 17.5cm baking tin.

Beat the egg yolks with the condensed milk, then drop tablespoons of the mixture into the blondie batter in the tin. Use the handle of a teaspoon to draw the condensed milk custard gently through, then arrange the roasted rhubarb on top, reserving the juice in the tin. Scatter over the hazelnuts.

Transfer the tin to the oven and bake for 15–20 minutes, until the top of the blondie looks just set. Let the blondie cool in the tin for 5 minutes before transferring it gently to a wire rack.

Serve warm or at room temperature, drizzled with the remaining rhubarb juice before serving. Store any leftovers in the fridge.

NOTE: you can use the remaining condensed milk in coffee, as they do in Vietnam.

FOR GLUTEN-FREE: substitute the flour with 75g ground almonds and 75g gluten-free flour (I like the brand Freee, from Doves Farm).

PISTACHIO & DATE BROWNIES

As you may have noticed in this book, I love using date syrup as a substitute for brown sugar – it's wonderful in its own right when you want a particularly date-like flavour, but has the added bonus of being diabetic-friendly. These sticky pistachio and date brownies are a moreish treat either way.

Serves: 8
Prep: 15 minutes
Cook: 15–18 minutes

85ml olive oil
125ml date syrup
50g diabetic-friendly
   dark chocolate
   (70% cocoa solids), broken
70ml milk
2 medium free-range eggs
40g cocoa powder
60g ground almonds
A pinch of sea salt flakes
100g soft pitted dates,
   roughly chopped
60g pistachios,
   roughly chopped

Preheat the oven to 160°C fan/180°C/gas 4. Measure the olive oil, date syrup and chocolate into a saucepan, then stir over a low heat until the chocolate has melted and the mixture is glossy.

Stir in the milk, then let the mixture cool for 5–10 minutes before whisking in the eggs.

Stir the cocoa powder, ground almonds and sea salt into the liquid mixture.

Pour the batter into a lined 24.5cm x 17.5cm baking tin, and scatter over the chopped dates and pistachios.

Transfer the tin to the oven and bake for 15–18 minutes, until the top of the brownie looks just set. Let the brownie cool in the tin for 5 minutes before transferring it gently to a wire rack.

Serve warm or at room temperature. This will keep well in an airtight container for 2–3 days.

BAKED MASCARPONE, CHERRY & WALNUT BROWNIES

The texture of these brownies is so light and fluffy that they definitely fall within the 'dessert' category rather than an afternoon snack – these would be a wonderful way to round off a dinner party, warm from the oven with an almost moussey texture from the swirled mascarpone. Leftovers (if any) are excellent for breakfast.

Serves: 8
Prep: 15 minutes
Cook: 20–25 minutes

85ml olive oil
125g soft dark brown sugar
50g dark chocolate
   (70% cocoa solids), chopped
90ml milk
2 medium free-range eggs
40g cocoa powder
60g ground almonds
A pinch of sea salt flakes
230g jarred black cherries in kirsch
   (drained weight)
150g mascarpone
50g chopped walnuts

Preheat the oven to 160°C fan/180°C/gas 4. Measure the olive oil, sugar and chocolate into a saucepan, then stir over a low heat until the chocolate has melted and the mixture is glossy.

Stir in 70ml of the milk, then let the mixture cool for 5–10 minutes before whisking in the eggs.

Stir the cocoa powder, ground almonds, sea salt and half the jarred cherries into the liquid mixture.

Beat the mascarpone with the remaining 20ml of milk until smooth, and set aside.

Pour the batter into a lined 24.5cm x 17.5cm baking tin, and drop in teaspoons of the beaten mascarpone. Use the handle of the teaspoon to draw the mascarpone gently through the chocolate mixture, then scatter over the remaining cherries and the chopped walnuts.

Transfer the tin to the oven and bake for 20–25 minutes, until the top of the brownie looks just set. Let the brownie cool in the tin for 5 minutes before transferring it gently to a wire rack.

Serve warm: if made in advance, you can gently reheat in the oven for 5 minutes at 160°C fan/180°C/gas 4. Store any leftovers in the fridge.

COOKIES

SALTED CHOCOLATE CHIP

(VEGAN)

CHOCOLATE, COCONUT & BRAZIL NUT

(VEGAN)

OLD-FASHIONED FRUIT & NUT

(VEGAN)

FIG, FENNEL & ORANGE

(VEGAN)

TRIPLE GINGER BISCUITS

(VEGAN)

SPELT, CHEDDAR & CARAWAY BISCUITS

(DIABETIC-FRIENDLY)

COOKIES

The cookies in this chapter remind me of the Millie's Cookies of my childhood – a beautifully soft texture, and wonderful eaten warm from the oven. The recipe is inspired by Ovenly's chocolate chip cookie recipe, with which I have mucked about, so all the recipes in the chapter are vegan, apart from the wildcard spelt, cheddar and caraway biscuits at the end, which I couldn't resist including.

There's only one thing to bear in mind with these cookie recipes – you really must rest the dough in the fridge for at least 1–2 hours to firm up; the wonderfully soft texture at the end is on account of the high liquid content, with the minor downside that the cookies therefore can't be shaped immediately. It's well worth the wait: once chilled, you can shape the cookies and then bake the lot at once, or bake half and freeze half, uncooked, to stick in the oven and bake as needed.

For the perfect soft-set cookie, I find 12 minutes in my oven at 155°C fan/175°C/ gas 3 works beautifully – the cookies will look a little pale, but continue to firm up as they cool on a wire rack. Your oven may run a little hotter or cooler, so you could take a preliminary look at 10 minutes, and leave them for up to 15, but you do want them as soft as possible while still being just cooked through, so feel free to scribble timing notes to suit your oven on the recipes that follow after a first test run.

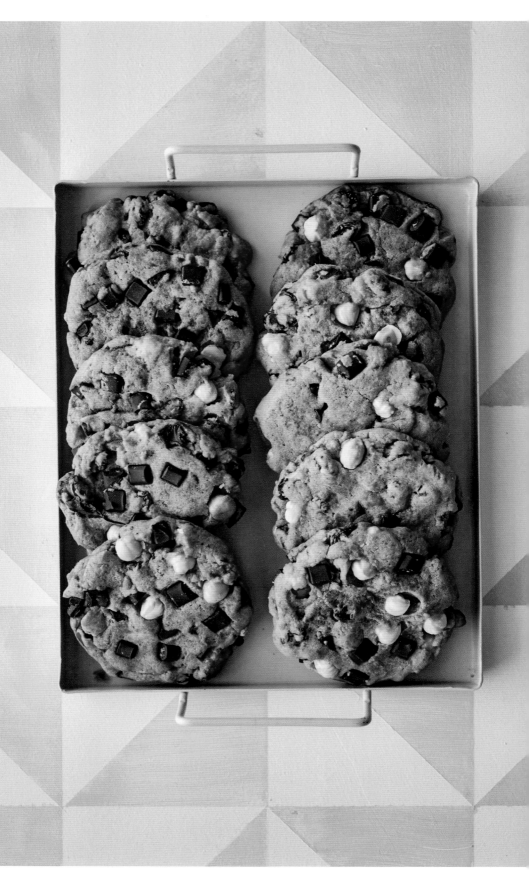

BASIC COOKIE

325g plain flour

1½ teaspoons baking powder

1 teaspoon sea salt flakes,
crumbled

170g soft light brown sugar

130ml olive oil

85ml water

GLUTEN-FREE COOKIE

325g gluten-free plain flour

1½ teaspoons baking powder

1 teaspoon sea salt flakes,
crumbled

170g soft light brown sugar

130ml olive oil

85ml water

DIABETIC-FRIENDLY COOKIE

325g plain flour

1½ teaspoons baking powder

1 teaspoon sea salt flakes,
crumbled

170ml date syrup

130ml olive oil

85ml water

ADDITIONAL INGREDIENTS

chopped nuts

chocolate chips

salt

raisins
or other dried fruit

lemon or orange zest

SALTED CHOCOLATE CHIP COOKIES

My friend Mitul introduced me to these cookies, to which he always adds grated orange zest – spectacularly good for fans of chocolate orange. This is the simplest version, but by all means add grated orange zest if you wish. As fans of Tony's Chocolonely bars will know, the salt makes these ridiculously addictive.

Makes:	12–15 cookies
Prep:	15 minutes
	+ 1–2 hours chilling
Cook:	12 minutes

325g plain flour
1½ teaspoons baking powder
1 teaspoon sea salt flakes,
    crumbled
100g vegan dark chocolate chips
    (70% cocoa solids)
    or 100g dark chocolate,
    chopped into small chunks
170g soft light brown sugar
130ml olive oil
85ml water
Sea salt flakes, to finish

FOR DIABETICS: replace the sugar with 170ml date syrup, and use a bar of diabetic-friendly dark chocolate, chopped into chunks.

FOR GLUTEN-FREE: replace the plain flour with gluten-free plain flour.

Stir the flour, baking powder, salt and dark chocolate chips or chunks together in a large bowl.

In another bowl, whisk the sugar, olive oil and water until smooth and completely incorporated – this will take a little time with a hand whisk, less with an electric whisk.

Stir the liquid ingredients with the dry ingredients until they come together into a sticky dough, then transfer the mix to the fridge to chill for 1–2 hours.

Once the dough has chilled, use an ice cream scoop to measure out 12–15 cookies on to a lined baking sheet, then use your hands to quickly pat them into neat, flat discs, leaving some space around the edges as they will expand. Scatter each cookie with a few sea salt flakes. (You can refrigerate them again for 30 minutes at this point, but I'm usually greedy and just get on with the baking.)

Preheat the oven to 155°C fan/175°C/gas 3, and when at temperature, transfer your cookies to the oven and bake for 12 minutes before removing the tray from the oven. They will look and feel very soft and be a very light colour, but don't worry, this is what you want.

Let the cookies cool on the baking sheet for 5 minutes, then carefully transfer them to a wire rack to cool a little more before eating. Once completely cool, you can store these in an airtight container for 3–4 days, or freeze and defrost as needed.

CHOCOLATE, COCONUT & BRAZIL NUT COOKIES

The coconut oil in these cookies, combined with the cocoa powder, turns them into something akin to Granny Boyd's biscuits in Nigella's *How to be a Domestic Goddess* – one of my favourite minimal-ingredient bakes. They have a thick, substantial mouthfeel – quite unlike ordinary cookies. I love them with a cup of tea (Earl Grey obvs).

Makes:	12–15 cookies
Prep:	15 minutes
	+ 1 hour chilling
Cook:	12 minutes

260g plain flour
40g cocoa powder
1½ teaspoons baking powder
½ teaspoon sea salt flakes,
   crumbled
50g vegan dark chocolate chips
   (70% cocoa solids)
   or 50g dark chocolate,
   chopped into small chunks
75g Brazil nuts, chopped
125g coconut oil
170g soft dark brown sugar
125ml water

Stir the flour, cocoa powder, baking powder, sea salt, chocolate chips and Brazil nuts together in a large bowl.

In a large saucepan, melt the coconut oil, then whisk in the sugar and water off the heat.

Stir the liquid ingredients into the dry ingredients – they will come together immediately into a dough. Flatten the dough into a disc, wrap it in clingfilm or a bag and transfer to the fridge to chill for 1 hour.

After 1 hour, break off 12–15 equal-sized pieces of dough and roll them between your hands, then flatten them into fat discs on a lined baking sheet – you want them about 1cm thick.

Preheat the oven to 155°C fan/175°C/gas 3. When at temperature, transfer the cookies to the oven and bake for 12 minutes. They will look soft, but will continue to firm up as they cool.

Leave the cookies on the baking sheet for 5 minutes, then carefully transfer to a wire rack to firm up. These will keep well in an airtight container for 2–3 days.

FOR DIABETICS: replace the sugar with 170ml date syrup, and use 50g diabetic-friendly dark chocolate, chopped into chunks.

FOR GLUTEN-FREE: replace the plain flour with gluten-free plain flour.

OLD-FASHIONED FRUIT & NUT COOKIES

Cadbury's Fruit and Nut bars are my parents' favourite. Apparently my mother craved them when she was expecting me, and my father would go and buy her large bars as a treat – which might explain my incurable sweet tooth. These cookies are my homage to the bar for them.

Makes: 12–15 cookies
Prep: 15 minutes
           + 1–2 hours chilling
Cook: 12–15 minutes

325g plain flour
1½ teaspoons baking powder
A pinch of sea salt flakes
200g vegan chocolate chips
    (milk and dark mixed)
    or 200g dark/milk chocolate
    bars, chopped into chunks
100g hazelnuts
100g raisins
170g soft dark brown sugar
130ml olive oil
85ml water

FOR DIABETICS: replace the sugar with 170ml date syrup, and use just one 100g bar of diabetic-friendly dark or milk chocolate, chopped into chunks.

FOR GLUTEN-FREE: replace the plain flour with gluten-free plain flour.

Stir the flour, baking powder, sea salt, chocolate chips or chunks, hazelnuts and raisins together in a large bowl.

In another bowl, whisk the sugar, olive oil and water until smooth and completely incorporated – this will take a little time with a hand whisk, less with an electric whisk.

Stir the liquid ingredients with the dry ingredients until they come together into a sticky dough, then transfer the mix to the fridge to chill for 1–2 hours.

Once the dough has chilled, use an ice cream scoop to measure out 12–15 cookies on to a lined baking sheet, then use your hands to quickly pat them into neat, flat discs, leaving some space around the edges as they will expand. (You can refrigerate them again for 30 minutes at this point, but I'm usually greedy and just get on with the baking.)

Preheat the oven to 155°C fan/175°C/gas 3; when at temperature, transfer your chilled or room temperature cookies to the oven and bake for 12–15 minutes. They will look and feel very soft, but don't worry, this is what you want.

Let the cookies cool on the baking sheet for 5 minutes, then carefully transfer them to a wire rack to cool a little more before eating.

Once completely cool, you can store these in an airtight container for 3–4 days, or freeze and defrost as needed.

FIG, FENNEL & ORANGE COOKIES

These are rather grown-up cookies – with a flavour reminiscent of fig rolls (which I have a particular fondness for). The fennel makes a nice, unusual contrast amid the sweetness, and works so well with the orange. Almost – but not quite – one of your five-a-day.

Makes: 12–15 cookies
Prep: 15 minutes
+ 1–2 hours chilling
Cook: 12 minutes

325g plain flour
1½ teaspoons baking powder
½ teaspoon sea salt flakes,
   crumbled
200g chopped dried figs
1 teaspoon fennel seeds,
   lightly crushed
1 unwaxed clementine, zest
   and juice
170g soft light brown sugar
130ml olive oil
55ml water

FOR DIABETICS: replace the soft light brown sugar with 170ml date syrup.

FOR GLUTEN-FREE: replace the plain flour with gluten-free plain flour.

Stir the flour, baking powder, sea salt, chopped figs and fennel seeds together in a large bowl.

In another bowl, whisk the clementine zest and juice, sugar, olive oil and water until smooth and completely incorporated – this will take a little time with a hand whisk, less with an electric whisk.

Stir the liquid ingredients with the dry ingredients until they come together into a sticky dough, then transfer the mix to the fridge to chill for 1–2 hours.

Once the dough has chilled, use an ice cream scoop to measure out 12–15 cookies on to a lined baking sheet, then use your hands to quickly pat them into neat, flat discs, leaving some space around the edges as they will expand. (You can refrigerate them again for 30 minutes at this point, but I'm usually greedy and just get on with the baking.)

Preheat the oven to 155°C fan/175°C/gas 3; when at temperature, transfer your chilled or room temperature cookies to the oven and bake for 12 minutes. They will look and feel very soft, but don't worry, this is what you want.

Let the cookies cool on the baking sheet for 5 minutes, then carefully transfer them to a wire rack to cool a little more before eating.

Once completely cool, you can store these in an airtight container for 3–4 days, or freeze and defrost as needed.

TRIPLE GINGER BISCUITS

Ginger biscuits are hands down my favourite type of biscuit. You can use stem ginger from a jar for these, or the crystallised kind for a textural contrast.

Makes: 12–15 cookies
Prep: 15 minutes
+ 1–2 hours chilling
Cook: 12 minutes

325g plain flour
1½ teaspoons baking powder
½ teaspoon sea salt flakes, crumbled
2 teaspoons grated fresh ginger
1 teaspoon ground ginger
60g stem ginger, chopped
170g soft dark brown sugar
130ml olive oil
85ml water

Stir the flour, baking powder, salt and the grated, ground and chopped stem ginger together in a large bowl.

In another bowl, whisk the sugar, olive oil and water until smooth and completely incorporated – this will take a little time with a hand whisk, less with an electric whisk.

Stir the liquid ingredients with the dry ingredients until they come together into a sticky dough, then transfer the mix to the fridge to chill for 1–2 hours.

Once the dough has chilled, use an ice cream scoop to measure out 12–15 cookies on to a lined baking sheet, then use your hands to quickly pat them into neat, flat discs, leaving some space around the edges as they will expand. (You can refrigerate them again for 30 minutes at this point, but I'm usually greedy and just get on with the baking.)

Preheat the oven to 155°C fan/175°C/gas 3; when at temperature, transfer your cookies into the oven and bake for 12 minutes for a Millie's Cookies-style soft set, or 15 minutes for a firmer, more biscuity set, before removing from the oven.

Let the cookies cool on the baking sheet for 5 minutes, then carefully transfer them to a wire rack to firm up.

FOR DIABETICS: omit the stem ginger, and use 170ml date syrup in place of the dark brown sugar.

FOR GLUTEN-FREE: replace the plain flour with gluten-free plain flour.

These will keep well in an airtight container for 3–4 days, or you can keep the dough in the fridge for up to 2 days and bake small batches as you need them.

SPELT, CHEDDAR & CARAWAY BISCUITS

This is something of a wildcard recipe: it doesn't follow the formula in the rest of the chapter – you stamp these biscuits out with cutters, and as you can see from the quantity of cheddar, it's unashamedly savoury. But I love it too much not to include it here – cut out small hearts or circles to go with pre-dinner drinks, or use fancy-shaped cutters for a cheese-snack menagerie.

Makes: a lot of biscuits
Prep: 15 minutes
            + 30 minutes chilling
Cook: 8–9 minutes

200g strong cheddar cheese,
    finely grated
100g spelt or plain flour,
    plus extra for dusting
1 teaspoon baking powder
1 teaspoon caraway seeds
2 teaspoons finely chopped
    rosemary
75g softened butter

Stir the grated cheddar, flour, baking powder, caraway seeds and chopped rosemary together in a large bowl.

Using your fingertips, gently work the butter into the flour and cheese until you have rubbly breadcrumbs (alternatively, you can blitz everything in a food processor until it looks like couscous).

Bring the crumbs together with your hands, and work very briefly to bring everything into a nice dough. Divide the dough in two, flatten each piece into a fat disc, then transfer to the fridge wrapped in clingfilm or in bags to chill for 30 minutes.

On a lightly floured surface, roll out the chilled dough to about 3mm thick, then stamp out shapes of your choice, transferring them to a lined baking sheet as you go. Reroll the scraps and keep stamping out until you've used up all the dough, then repeat with the remaining disc of dough from the fridge. You may need to use two baking sheets, depending on size.

Preheat the oven to 180°C fan/200°C/gas 6; once at temperature, transfer the biscuits to the oven and bake for 8–9 minutes, until golden brown – they will continue to firm up, so don't worry that they look a little soft.

Transfer to a wire rack and let the biscuits cool a little before tucking in. Perfect with a glass of wine – any leftovers keep well in an airtight container for 2–3 days.

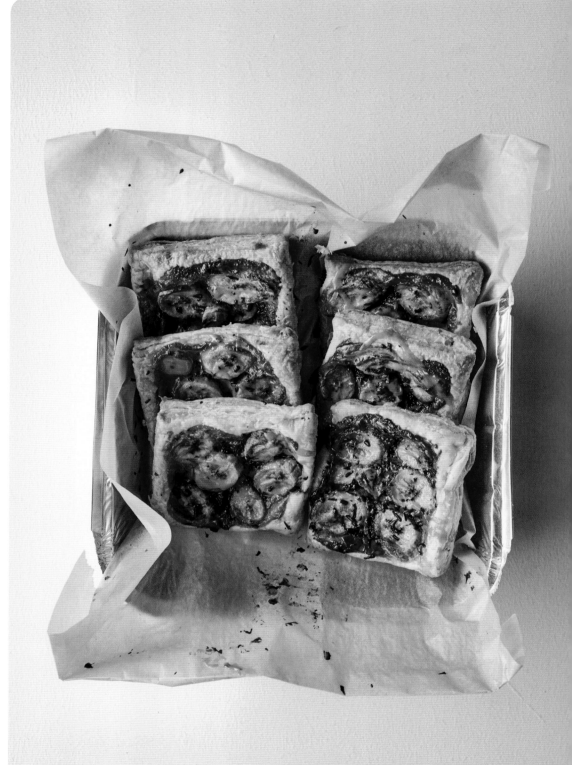

CRUMBLES, TARTS & COBBLERS

BANOFFEE CHOCOLATE TARTS

PLUM, CHERRY & CINNAMON COBBLER

PEACH, GINGER & ALMOND CRUMBLE

RHUBARB & VANILLA TART

PEAR, BLACKBERRY & CARDAMOM CRUMBLE

APPLE, CHEDDAR & CLOVE GALETTE

CRUMBLES, TARTS & COBBLERS

Fresh fruit is such a lovely baking ingredient – when you've got a glut of apples, pears and plums and have had your fill of eating them raw, there's nothing nicer – or indeed easier – than sticking them under a crumble topping. Cobblers, which are next door to crumbles and scones in terms of ingredients, provide a fun crazy paving-style topping for baked fruit, and galettes are an easy, no-fuss pastry base for home-made tarts. (Mine always look rustic but this is part of their charm.)

This chapter is all about easy fruit-based puddings: you can mix and match the fillings or toppings as you wish. The plum, cherry and cinnamon cobbler on page 116 would work just as well with a crumble topping, and the pear, blackberry and cardamom crumble on page 122 would work wonderfully in a galette.

And importantly, pretty much all of them would work for one of my favourite types of dessert: using bought puff pastry as a base and arranging the ingredients on top in an attractive way, as with the rhubarb and vanilla tart on page 120 or the banoffee chocolate tarts on page 114.

You'll find my basic crumble, cobbler and galette recipes overleaf.

BASIC CRUMBLE

50g plain or spelt flour

50g soft light brown sugar

50g oats

50g unsalted butter

50g flaked almonds

BASIC COBBLER

250g self-raising flour

1½ teaspoons cream of tartar

1 teaspoon baking powder

50g caster sugar

40g unsalted butter

120ml milk

1 medium free-range egg,
lightly beaten

Demerara sugar, to scatter

BASIC GALETTE

250g plain or spelt flour

175g cold cubed butter

50g caster sugar

VEGAN, GLUTEN-FREE & DIABETIC ADAPTATIONS

To veganise crumbles or galettes:
replace the butter with olive oil,
coconut oil
or a plant-based spread.

**For gluten-free
(for crumbles and cobblers only)**:
replace the flour with gluten-free
and use gluten-free oats.

For diabetics: replace the 50g
sugar with 25g xylitol.

BANOFFEE CHOCOLATE TARTS

This is unashamedly indulgent – something to make and eat occasionally, if enthusiastically. I just about resisted the urge to increase the calorie content by adding peanut butter: very restrained.

Makes: 6
Prep: 15 minutes
Cook: 25–30 minutes

1 sheet of ready-rolled puff pastry,
    cut into 6 squares
200g caramel (tinned
    or dulce de leche)
50g dark chocolate
    (70% cocoa solids), grated
3–4 large bananas,
    sliced into coins
2 tablespoons melted butter
Chocolate sauce, to serve
    (optional)

Preheat the oven to 180°C fan/200°C/gas 6. Lay the squares of pastry on a lined baking sheet, and spread a tablespoon of caramel evenly over each square, leaving a 1cm border around the edge. Reserve the remaining caramel.

Scatter the grated chocolate over the caramel, and arrange the banana coins all over the top. Brush with the melted butter, then drizzle over the remaining caramel.

Transfer the tarts to the oven and bake for 25–30 minutes, until the edges are golden brown and crisp. Serve hot, drizzled with chocolate sauce if you wish.

FOR GLUTEN-FREE: use gluten-free ready-rolled puff pastry.

PLUM, CHERRY & CINNAMON COBBLER

This is such a lovely, rich combination of fruit – I'm usually very sparing with cinnamon when baking (or cooking, for that matter), but here, the robust cherries and plums stand up well to the flavour. A nice autumnal dessert – perfect with clotted cream or crème fraîche on the side.

Serves: 6–8
Prep: 20 minutes
Cook: 30 minutes

350g fresh cherries,
   stoned and halved
7 ripe plums, stoned and quartered
80g soft dark brown sugar
1 teaspoon ground cinnamon
250g self-raising flour
1½ teaspoons cream of tartar
1 teaspoon baking powder
50g caster sugar
40g unsalted butter
120ml milk
1 medium free-range egg,
   lightly beaten
Demerara sugar, to scatter

Preheat the oven to 180°C fan/200°C/gas 6. Tip the cherries, plums, dark brown sugar and cinnamon into a 20cm x 25cm roasting tin, mix well, then set aside.

Measure the flour, cream of tartar, baking powder, caster sugar and butter into the bowl of a food processor and blitz until it comes together sandily. Add the milk a little at a time until it just comes together into a dough. (Alternatively, work the dry ingredients and butter with your fingertips until sandy in texture, then add the milk a little at a time.)

Divide the dough into 16 small portions – these can be fairly rough, not perfect-looking – and dot them over the fruit in the roasting tin. Brush the dough with the egg, scatter with demerara sugar, then transfer to the oven and bake for 30 minutes.

Serve warm, with crème fraîche or clotted cream alongside if you wish.

PEACH, GINGER & ALMOND CRUMBLE

Fresh peaches can take a surprising amount of sugar, but they work so well with ginger in this simple crumble recipe that it's hard to begrudge them. I like to use spelt flour here for a slightly different flavour, but by all means use ordinary flour if that's what you have in.

Serves: 6
Prep: 15 minutes
Cook: 35–40 minutes

350g fresh peaches,
   stoned and quartered
100g caster sugar
10g fresh ginger, grated
50g spelt flour
50g soft light brown sugar
50g oats
50g cold cubed butter
50g flaked almonds

Preheat the oven to 160°C fan/180°C/gas 4. Tip the peaches, caster sugar and ginger into a 25cm x 19cm roasting tin and mix gently.

Measure the flour, brown sugar, oats, cold cubed butter and flaked almonds into a large bowl. With your fingertips, gently work together into a rubbly crumble mix – it should look a bit like almond granola by the time you're done (albeit stickier).

Scatter the crumble over the peaches, then transfer to the oven and bake for 35–40 minutes, until the fruit is cooked through, and the topping is golden brown and crisp.

Serve hot. (Leftovers keep well in the fridge and can be reheated in the microwave or oven.)

FOR GLUTEN-FREE: replace the spelt flour with gluten-free flour, and use gluten-free oats.

RHUBARB & VANILLA TART

I could eat this beautifully pink rhubarb tart any time of the day – it's sharp, sweet and mildly addictive. What you gain from a lovely parquet pattern on top, you lose slightly in terms of the crispness of the pastry, so by all means cut your pastry into four smaller rectangles for individual tarts if you wish.

Serves: 4–6
Prep: 15 minutes
Cook: 25–30 minutes

400g pink rhubarb
65g soft light brown sugar
½ teaspoon vanilla extract
    or scraped seeds from
    ¼ vanilla pod
25g pine nuts,
    very finely chopped or ground
2 teaspoons cornflour
1 sheet of ready-rolled
    puff pastry

Preheat the oven to 180°C fan/200°C/gas 6. Cut the rhubarb into 2.5cm pieces, then mix with 40g of the soft light brown sugar and the vanilla extract or seeds and set aside.

In a separate bowl, mix the chopped or ground pine nuts with the remaining 25g of soft light brown sugar and the cornflour.

Lay the pastry out on a baking sheet, using the paper it comes wrapped in as a liner, and cut off 8cm from the bottom of the pastry: reserve for another use.

Spread the pine nut mixture all over the pastry, leaving a 2.5cm border around the edges.

Arrange the rhubarb in a parquet pattern as opposite, or in a pattern of your choice – it's a little tricky to start with, but once you get going it's easier.

Transfer the tart to the oven and bake for 25–30 minutes, until the pastry is golden brown and crisp and the rhubarb is cooked through.

Serve immediately.

FOR GLUTEN-FREE: use gluten-free ready-rolled puff pastry.

PEAR, BLACKBERRY & CARDAMOM CRUMBLE

Black pepper might seem like an unusual addition to this crumble, but it works beautifully with the pears, blackberries and cardamom. As good for breakfast as it is for dessert.

Serves: 6
Prep: 15 minutes
Cook: 40 minutes

6 ripe pears (approx. 600g),
  cored and chopped
  into small pieces (1.5cm)
½ teaspoon black peppercorns,
  ground
6 green cardamom pods,
  seeds ground
40g golden syrup or honey
100g blackberries, halved if large
50g plain flour
50g soft dark brown sugar
50g oats
50g cold cubed butter

Preheat the oven to 160°C fan/180°C/gas 4. If your pears aren't ripe, soften them in a pan for 10 minutes with the syrup or honey and spices. Otherwise, tip the pears, black pepper, ground cardamom, syrup or honey and blackberries into a smallish roasting tin (approx. 30cm x 20cm), and mix gently.

Measure the flour, sugar, oats and cold cubed butter into a large bowl and with your fingertips gently work together into a rubbly crumble mix – it should look a bit like granola by the time you're done (albeit stickier).

Scatter the crumble over the fruit, then transfer to the oven and bake for 40 minutes, until the fruit is cooked through and the topping is golden brown and crisp.

Serve hot. (Leftovers keep well in the fridge and can be reheated in the microwave or oven.)

FOR GLUTEN-FREE: replace the plain flour with gluten-free flour, and use gluten-free oats.

APPLE, CHEDDAR & CLOVE GALETTE

Freeform galettes are one of the easiest types of tart you can make – the dough is wonderfully forgiving. I'd venture to say that this apple and cheddar galette is even better if you leave it in the fridge overnight once cooked, and warm it up to serve the next day. Any canines in the house will undoubtedly turn up at the scent of hot apples and melted cheese, but cloves aren't suitable for dogs, so this is sadly not shareable.

Serves: 8
Prep: 20 minutes
+ 1 hour chilling
Cook: 30–35 minutes

DOUGH
250g spelt flour
175g cold cubed butter
50g caster sugar

FILLING
3 dessert apples, ideally
    Pink Lady, finely sliced
7 cloves, ground
40g soft dark brown sugar
80g sharp cheddar, grated
2 sprigs of rosemary,
    needles chopped
20g butter, cubed
1 medium free-range egg yolk,
    beaten

For the galette dough, blitz the spelt flour, butter and caster sugar in a food processor, then add a little cold water, a tablespoon at a time, just until everything comes together into a dough. (Alternatively, work together with your fingertips until sandy in texture, then add the water sparingly and bring together into a dough.) Wrap the dough in clingfilm and transfer to the fridge to chill for 1 hour. Mix the apples, ground cloves and dark brown sugar together and set aside.

After 1 hour, preheat the oven to 180°C fan/200°C/gas 6. Roll out the dough on a lined baking sheet to an approx. 30cm circle – don't worry about messy edges. Scatter the grated cheese over the middle of the pastry, leaving a 5cm border all around.

Arrange the apples over the cheese as you wish, keeping to within the 5cm border, and scatter over the rosemary. Bring the edges of the pastry up over the apples to just enclose the filling, as opposite.

Dot the apples with the butter, brush the exposed dough with the egg yolk, then transfer to the oven and bake for 30–35 minutes.

Let the galette cool on the baking sheet for 5 minutes, then carefully transfer to a wire rack to cool down. If you can, let it cool completely before refrigerating and serve warm the next day; the flavour is really incredible.

BREAD
& BUTTER
PUDDINGS

CHOCOLATE BREAD & BUTTER
PUDDING

COFFEE & WALNUT
CROISSANT PUDDING

AMARETTO PANETTONE
BREAD & BUTTER PUDDING

ORANGE CHOCOLATE CHIP
BREAD & BUTTER PUDDING

STICKY TOFFEE
BRIOCHE PUDDING
(DIABETIC-FRIENDLY)

PISTACHIO PAIN AU CHOCOLAT
PUDDING

BREAD & BUTTER PUDDINGS

Bread disappears in my house. Forget 'bread and butter puddings are a fantastic way to use up leftover bread' – there are rarely, if ever, any leftover slices to go into a pudding. When I want to make one, I buy a loaf of soft white farmhouse just for that purpose; it's tempting to put a label on it 'FOR PUDDING USE' so it doesn't disappear under thick wodges of salted butter to be eaten standing up at the counter.

The perfect bread and butter pudding to me has a good ratio of crisp on the top, with a meltingly soft inside: perhaps epitomised by the orange chocolate chip version on page 136. Then there's the favourite of my childhood, a chocolate bread and butter pudding like the one on page 130, and the more recent 'fancy versions' with what is in essence pre-buttered bread – brioche, croissants and pain au chocolat.

I can't think of an easier pudding, given that all you need to do is whisk some egg yolks, sugar and cream together: my favourite quick custard recipe, on which the recipes in this chapter are based, is below.

BASIC CUSTARD

3 medium free-range egg yolks

50g caster sugar

300ml single cream

50ml milk (or booze, or coffee)

This amount of custard should do you for:

4 pains au chocolat,

4 croissants,

or 300g soft white farmhouse bread

NOTES

If you have more bread to use up, just increase the cream or milk – you want a squashy texture going into the oven.

For diabetics:
you can replace the sugar with 50ml of date syrup, but at the risk of sounding like Marie Antoinette, discuss brioche and croissants with your GP first.

CHOCOLATE BREAD & BUTTER PUDDING

My favourite type of bread and butter pudding – rich and indulgent, and perfect to round off a dinner party, if you can manage not to eat it all before your guests arrive. You could serve it with raspberries as well as the crème fraîche if you wish.

Serves: 8
Prep: 10 minutes
            + 45 minutes sitting
Cook: 25–30 minutes

400ml single cream
100ml milk
200g dark chocolate
    (70% cocoa solids), chopped
4 medium free-range egg yolks
A pinch of sea salt flakes
60g soft dark brown sugar
450g soft white sliced
    farmhouse bread, buttered
    (crusts removed if you wish)
2 tablespoons demerara sugar
Crème fraîche, to serve (optional)

Heat the single cream and milk in a saucepan until it just comes to the boil, then pour it over the chopped chocolate in a heatproof bowl. Leave to sit for 2 minutes, then whisk until the chocolate has melted.

Whisk the egg yolks, salt and dark brown sugar into the chocolate cream until combined.

Cut the buttered bread into quarters and arrange one layer in a buttered 20cm x 26cm roasting tin. Spoon over enough chocolate custard to coat generously, squashing down the bread well with a spoon, then repeat, layering up the bread and custard until you've used up all the bread. Pour the remaining custard over the top, squash everything down again gently, and leave to sit for 45 minutes.

Ten minutes before you're ready to cook, preheat the oven to 150°C fan/170°C/gas 3. Scatter the top of the pudding with the demerara sugar, then transfer to the oven and bake for 25–30 minutes, until crisp on top, but still soft within.

Serve hot, with crème fraîche alongside if you wish.

FOR GLUTEN-FREE: use gluten-free sliced bread.

COFFEE & WALNUT CROISSANT PUDDING

Coffee and croissants are an ideal breakfast, and combine beautifully here if you have a few knocking about. Nursery food with an adult twist.

Serves: 6
Prep: 10 minutes
Cook: 25–30 minutes

3 medium free-range egg yolks
50g caster sugar
300ml single cream
50ml milk
50ml strong black coffee
4 leftover croissants
50g walnuts, finely chopped
2 tablespoons demerara sugar
Icing sugar, for dusting

Preheat the oven to 150°C fan/170°C/gas 3. Whisk the egg yolks with the caster sugar, then slowly whisk in the single cream, milk and coffee. Set aside.

Slice or tear up the croissants and arrange in a buttered 20cm x 26cm roasting tin.

Pour the coffee custard mixture over the croissants, squashing them down well, then scatter over the walnuts and demerara sugar. Transfer to the oven and bake for 25–30 minutes, until crisp and golden brown on top, but still soft within.

Dust with icing sugar and serve hot. If you have leftovers, this reheats very well in the microwave for breakfast the next day.

FOR GLUTEN-FREE: use gluten-free croissants.

AMARETTO PANETTONE
BREAD & BUTTER PUDDING

There always seems to be a panettone knocking about under the Christmas tree, and my favourite thing to do is make it into a rich, indulgent bread and butter pudding – perfect for a cold night. I love the flexibility of this recipe – serve with brandy butter if you have it about, or use Baileys or your favourite Christmas drink to replace the amaretto.

Serves:	6
Prep:	10 minutes
Cook:	25 minutes

100ml amaretto
100g raisins
3 medium free-range egg yolks
50g caster sugar
300ml single cream
1 x 750g panettone
Icing sugar, to serve

Preheat the oven to 150°C fan/170°C/gas 3. Heat the amaretto in a small saucepan until just under boiling, then turn off the heat and add the raisins. Stir, then leave them to marinate.

Whisk the egg yolks with the caster sugar, then slowly whisk in the single cream. Set aside.

Cut the panettone into quarters, and cut each quarter into 1.5cm slices. Arrange the slices in a 20cm x 26cm roasting tin

Pour two-thirds of the custard mixture over the panettone, squashing it down well, then scatter over the raisins and warm amaretto. Pour over the rest of the custard, squashing the panettone down gently. Transfer to the oven and bake for 25 minutes, until golden brown on top, but still soft within.

Dust with icing sugar and serve hot. If you have leftovers, this reheats very well in the microwave for a slightly boozy breakfast the next day.

ORANGE CHOCOLATE CHIP
BREAD & BUTTER PUDDING

This is based on a favourite steamed pudding – orange chocolate chip –
which my mother made for us as children. This bread and butter version uses
the same flavourings but helps if you've got some leftover bread to use up.

Serves: 6
Prep: 10 minutes
Cook: 25–30 minutes

3 medium free-range egg yolks
50g caster sugar
1 orange, zest and juice
300ml single cream
50ml milk
300g soft white sliced farmhouse
    bread, buttered
100g dark chocolate
    (70% cocoa solids),
    cut into chunks
Custard, to serve (optional)

Preheat the oven to 150°C fan/170°C/gas 3. Whisk the egg yolks with the caster sugar and orange zest, then slowly whisk in the single cream, milk and orange juice. Set aside.

Cut the buttered bread into quarters and arrange one layer in a buttered 20cm x 26cm roasting tin. Spoon over enough orange custard to coat, squashing down the bread well with a spoon, then scatter over a layer of chocolate chunks. Repeat, layering up the bread, chocolate chunks and custard until you've used up all the bread. Pour the remaining custard over the top, add a final layer of chocolate chunks, and gently squash everything down again.

Transfer the pudding to the oven and bake for 25–30 minutes, until crisp and golden brown on top, but still soft within.

Serve hot, with custard on the side if you wish.

FOR GLUTEN-FREE: use gluten-free sliced bread.

STICKY TOFFEE BRIOCHE PUDDING

Packed with jammy dates, this dessert is lightly inspired by a sticky toffee pudding rather than a full-on version: perfect for a late breakfast or brunch.

Serves: 6
Prep: 10 minutes
Cook: 25–30 minutes

3 medium free-range egg yolks
50ml date syrup
   (or 50g soft dark brown sugar)
300ml single cream
200ml whole milk
400g sliced or torn brioche
250g soft pitted dates, chopped
Date syrup, to serve (optional)

Preheat the oven to 150°C fan/170°C/gas 3. Whisk the egg yolks with the date syrup or soft dark brown sugar, then slowly whisk in the single cream and milk. Set aside.

Arrange the sliced or torn brioche in a buttered 20cm x 26cm roasting tin, tucking the dates in between the pieces of brioche.

Pour the custard mixture over the brioche, squashing the slices down well, then transfer to the oven and bake for 25–30 minutes, until crisp and golden brown on top, but still soft within.

Serve hot, with a drizzle of date syrup if you wish.

PISTACHIO PAIN AU CHOCOLAT PUDDING

This indulgent pain au chocolat pudding is as good to finish off a dinner party as it is for breakfast the next day, with a rich, pistachio-enriched custard running through the dish. As the pain au chocolat has a high butter content, you can skip the usual buttering of each slice.

Serves: 6
Prep: 10 minutes
Cook: 25–30 minutes

100g pistachios
3 medium free-range egg yolks
50g caster sugar
300ml single cream
50ml milk
4 pains au chocolat

Preheat the oven to 150°C fan/170°C/gas 3. Use a food processor or spice grinder to briefly blitz 50g of the pistachios into a rough powder – don't overblitz, or they'll get oily. Roughly chop the remaining pistachios and set aside.

Whisk the egg yolks with the caster sugar, then slowly whisk in the single cream, milk and ground pistachios.

Slice each pain au chocolat into three pieces and arrange in a buttered 20cm x 26cm roasting tin.

Pour the pistachio custard mixture over the sliced pain au chocolat, squashing the slices down well, then scatter over the chopped pistachios. Transfer to the oven and bake for 25–30 minutes, until crisp and golden brown on top, but still soft within. Serve.

FOR GLUTEN-FREE: use gluten-free pains au chocolat.

MINIMAL BAKING

MARSHMALLOW, PEANUT
& CHOCOLATE CORNFLAKE CUPS

CHOCOLATE, CHERRY
& PISTACHIO FRIDGE CAKE

MINI'S PEANUT BUTTER CUPS
(VEGAN, GLUTEN-FREE)

MAPLE PECAN FLAPJACKS

CRANBERRY ALMOND
FLAPJACKS
(VEGAN)

CHOCOLATE LEMON MASCARPONE
CHEESECAKE

MINIMAL BAKING

FRIDGE BARS, FLAPJACKS, BAKING WITH CHILDREN

This chapter is something of a nod to the sort of thing I liked to make as a child – flapjacks, chocolate tiffin, cornflake cakes – all easy to stir together, with only the flapjacks requiring a stint in the oven. It's hard to beat my mother's tiffin, but the chocolate, cherry and pistachio fridge cake on page 148 is a worthy contender, wonderful with a cup of coffee.

My first *Roasting Tin* book contained my favourite simple flapjack recipe, which I have adapted here for two marginally more healthy versions, as I believe children nowadays aren't handed tubs of golden syrup to play with. Maple syrup provides a wonderful smoky note in the maple pecan flapjacks on page 152, and the cranberry almond flapjacks on page 154 are brilliant as an on-the-go snack. I have suggested using agave syrup, as it feels rather virtuous, but you could certainly use golden syrup if that's what you have in the cupboard.

The chocolate lemon cheesecake on page 156 is a slightly more grown-up addition, but I couldn't write a minimal baking chapter without including at least one cheesecake. Mascarpone and chocolate above a layer of lemon curd might sound unusual, but it may be my proudest creation.

While I haven't included templates as with the other chapters in the book, the recipes are easily adaptable – the peanut butter cups on page 150 would work just as well with almond butter, and you could substitute your preferred nuts in the marshmallow peanut cups on page 146: a storecupboard raid and using up what you have is often an excellent start to an afternoon's baking.

MARSHMALLOW, PEANUT
& CHOCOLATE CORNFLAKE CUPS

It's hard to improve on the classic chocolate cornflake cup, but in the interests of experimentation, I came up with this one – somewhere between a cornflake cup and a rocky road, with sticky marshmallows and a hit of salt from the peanuts. Easy to make with children, and good enough that you'll want a few for yourself.

Makes: 12 ordinary
            or 24 mini-muffin
            cups
Prep: 15 minutes
Set: 30–40 minutes

200g chocolate
  (54% cocoa solids),
  roughly broken
50g salted peanuts
60g mini marshmallows
  (vegetarian)
80g cornflakes
A pinch of sea salt flakes

TO FINISH
A handful of salted peanuts,
  finely chopped
A handful of mini marshmallows
  (vegetarian), finely chopped

You will need a 24-cup mini-muffin tin or a 12-cup fairy cake tin, lightly oiled.

Melt the chocolate in 20-second blasts in the microwave, stirring in between, until smooth and glossy.

Stir in the peanuts, mini marshmallows and cornflakes with a wooden spoon, turning the mixture thoroughly until everything is well coated in the chocolate. The marshmallows may melt a bit – that's fine.

Scatter in the sea salt and give the mix one last turn, then use a spoon to divide it evenly between your 24- or 12-cup tin. Once you're done, use the spoon to gently press down on the mix – you don't want to squash the cornflakes, as the air pockets are arguably the best bits, but use just a bit of light pressure to pack them in.

Scatter over the remaining finely chopped peanuts and mini marshmallows, then transfer to the fridge to set for 30–40 minutes. Use a rounded knife to loosen the cups, then eat, serve or store in an airtight container for up to a week.

CHOCOLATE, CHERRY & PISTACHIO FRIDGE CAKE

A fridge cake fit for a queen: this tiffin combines all my favourite ingredients – glacé cherries, chocolate, pistachios and golden syrup.

Serves: 8
Prep: 10 minutes
Set: 3 hours

100g salted butter
200g dark chocolate
  (70% cocoa solids),
  roughly chopped
70g golden syrup
200g digestive biscuits,
  roughly broken
200g glacé cherries, halved
100g whole pistachios,
  roughly chopped

In a large saucepan, melt the butter, chocolate and golden syrup over a low heat, stirring continuously until smoothly melted, then turn off the heat.

Reserve a heaped tablespoon each of the broken digestives, glacé cherries and pistachios – you're going to use them to decorate later – and tip the rest into the saucepan with the chocolate mixture. Stir gently to coat, then transfer the mix to a lined 26.5cm x 19cm roasting tin.

Put the tin into the fridge, and leave to set for an hour, then scatter over the reserved broken biscuits, cherries and pistachios.

Return the tin to the fridge to set for a further 2 hours before slicing and serving.

TO VEGANISE: substitute the butter for 100g coconut oil and a pinch of salt and use vegan dark chocolate.

FOR GLUTEN-FREE: use gluten-free digestive biscuits.

MINI'S PEANUT BUTTER CUPS

A lovely treat/high-energy snack to have in the fridge – these are so quick and easy to put together. If cooking with children, you could substitute the dark chocolate with a good-quality milk chocolate.

Makes: 12
Prep: 10 minutes
Set: 1 hour 30 minutes

100g crunchy peanut butter
15g coconut oil
A pinch of ground cinnamon
75g dark chocolate
   (70% cocoa solids), chopped
Sea salt flakes

Melt the peanut butter and coconut oil with the cinnamon in a saucepan over a low heat, stirring continuously.

Divide the mixture equally between 12 mini-muffin or fairy cake tins, making sure to leave a 2–3mm space at the top for the chocolate.

Transfer the tin to the freezer to chill for 30 minutes.

Melt the dark chocolate in a heatproof bowl set over a pan of simmering water (don't let the base of the bowl touch the water). Once the peanut butter cups have had 30 minutes in the freezer, divide the chocolate equally between the cups, finishing with a scatter of sea salt flakes. Return the tin to the freezer to set for 1 hour.

After 1 hour, use a knife to gently remove the cups from the tin: they should slide out easily. Allow to sit at room temperature for 10 minutes before serving, and store in the fridge to snack on as needed.

FOR DIABETICS: use a good brand of diabetic-friendly dark chocolate (70% cocoa solids).

MAPLE PECAN FLAPJACKS

While I love golden syrup in a flapjack, maple syrup gives a wonderful flavour here, and works beautifully with the pecans. Do use ordinary small oats for this rather than jumbo oats – they hold together better in the finished flapjack.

Serves: 9
Prep: 10 minutes
Cook: 25–30 minutes

150ml maple syrup
100g caster sugar
150g unsalted butter
250g porridge oats
   (not jumbo oats)
100g pecans, roughly broken
A shake of ground cinnamon

Preheat the oven to 150°C fan/170°C/gas 3. Melt the maple syrup, caster sugar and butter together over a medium heat and stir until smoothly amalgamated, then pour into a bowl with the porridge oats, broken pecans and cinnamon.

Mix thoroughly until the oats are completely coated in the butter mix, then transfer to a lined approx. 30cm x 20cm roasting tin. Pat down well with a large fish slice or the back of a tablespoon, then bake in the oven for 25–30 minutes, until just firm to the touch.

Let the flapjack cool in the tin for 10 minutes, then score out the slices with a sharp knife. Once they've had a little more time to cool, finish cutting the flapjack into pieces, and serve warm or at room temperature.

Leftovers, once completely cold, will keep well in an airtight container for 3–4 days.

FOR GLUTEN-FREE: use gluten-free oats.

CRANBERRY ALMOND FLAPJACKS

A breakfast-style flapjack packed with fruit and nuts for when you're on the go, but want something nutritious and not overly sugary to take with you.

Serves: 8
Prep: 10 minutes
Cook: 25–30 minutes

200ml agave syrup
115g coconut oil
100g pitted soft dates,
   chopped
250g porridge oats
   (not jumbo oats)
100g flaked almonds
150g dried cranberries
1 teaspoon ground ginger

Preheat the oven to 150°C fan/170°C/gas 3. Melt the agave syrup and coconut oil together over a medium heat with the dates, then pour into a bowl with the porridge oats, flaked almonds, dried cranberries and ground ginger.

Mix thoroughly until the oats are completely coated in the agave mix, then transfer to a lined 26.5cm x 19cm roasting tin. Pat down well with a large fish slice or the back of a tablespoon, then bake in the oven for 25–30 minutes, until just firm to the touch.

Let the flapjack cool in the tin for 10 minutes, then score out the slices with a sharp knife. Once they've had a little more time to cool, finish cutting the flapjack into pieces and serve warm or at room temperature.

Leftovers, once completely cold, will keep well in an airtight container for 3–4 days.

FOR GLUTEN-FREE: use gluten-free oats.

CHOCOLATE LEMON MASCARPONE CHEESECAKE

This cheesecake is enough to convert the most hardened cheesecake avoider (me) to someone who dives into the fridge with a spoon for just one more bite. I love the freshness of the zingy lemon curd against the chocolate mascarpone base – rich, indulgent and very moreish.

Serves: 8–10
Prep: 10 minutes
Set: overnight

150g chocolate digestive biscuits
60g unsalted butter, melted
250g mascarpone cheese,
  at room temperature
250g full-fat Philadelphia cheese,
  at room temperature
300g dark chocolate
  (70% cocoa solids)
25g honey
150g lemon curd

Blitz the digestive biscuits in a food processor (or smash them in a bag, using a rolling pin) until fine. Mix with the melted butter, then pat down evenly over the lined base of a 20cm springform cake tin. Transfer to the fridge to set.

Whisk the mascarpone and Philadelphia together until smooth and set aside.

Melt the dark chocolate in a heatproof bowl set over a pan of simmering water (don't let the base of the bowl touch the boiling water). Turn off the heat.

Whisk 2 heaped tablespoons of the mascarpone mix into the chocolate; once incorporated, add the rest a few tablespoons at a time, along with the honey, until smoothly mixed: do this quite quickly, as the chocolate will want to set – a vigorous beating will bring it all together smoothly.

Spread the lemon curd all over the chilled biscuit base, then add heaped tablespoons of the chocolate mixture over the top and smooth it down evenly. Return the tin to the fridge to set overnight.

To unmould, carefully run a hot knife around the edges of the springform tin, then remove the sides. Let the cheesecake sit for 10 minutes at room temperature before serving.

FOR GLUTEN-FREE: use gluten-free digestive biscuits.

CUPCAKES

LAVENDER

ROSE & PISTACHIO

(GLUTEN-FREE)

BLACK FOREST

ROSEMARY & LEMON CURD

PINEAPPLE & COCONUT

(GLUTEN-FREE)

RASPBERRY BAKEWELL

(GLUTEN-FREE)

CUPCAKES

I can't get over my childlike enthusiasm for cupcakes – they take just minutes to put together and bake, and feel disproportionately pleasing to eat in just a couple of bites. The cakes in this chapter are the old-fashioned fairy cake style, which is to say flat on top, and with just a little glacé icing. (Though if I am baking for myself, I would almost always forgo the icing and just eat them plain.) If you are fond of buttercream, it's helpful to know that you need twice as much icing sugar as softened butter, and that this can be made very quickly in a food processor.

The template for these recipes is the same as for the traybake cakes in the first chapter, but with smaller proportions – by all means double up if you're making cupcakes en masse. This quantity is enough for 12 generously filled muffin-sized cupcakes – you will get a few more if you are using smaller fairy cake cases and shallow tins.

BASIC CUPCAKE

115g softened unsalted butter

115g sugar (caster, golden caster, soft light or dark brown)

2 medium free-range eggs

115g self-raising flour

1 teaspoon baking powder

BASIC GLUTEN-FREE CUPCAKE

115g softened unsalted butter

115g sugar (caster, golden caster, soft light or dark brown)

2 medium free-range eggs

115g gluten-free self-raising flour (or a mixture of gluten-free self-raising flour and ground almonds, pistachios or hazelnuts)

1 teaspoon baking powder

40ml milk

LAVENDER CUPCAKES

I couldn't have a cupcake chapter without including a recipe for lavender, my friend Christine's favourite. If you grow your own lavender on a balcony or in a garden, this is a perfect way to use it up at the end of the season – these are lovely, light floral cakes.

Makes: 12
Prep: 10 minutes
Cook: 15 minutes

115g softened unsalted butter
115g caster sugar
2 heaped teaspoons crushed
   edible lavender
2 medium free-range eggs
115g self-raising flour
1 teaspoon baking powder

ICING
200g icing sugar
30ml water
A dab of Grape Violet food
   colouring
12 sprigs of lavender

Preheat the oven to 160°C fan/180°C/gas 4. Whisk the butter and sugar together with the crushed lavender until pale and fluffy, then beat in the eggs one at a time.

Gently fold in the self-raising flour and baking powder, taking care not to overmix. Divide the batter equally between 12 paper cases in a cupcake or muffin tin.

Transfer the cakes to the oven and bake for 15 minutes, until firm to the touch and a skewer inserted comes out clean.

Leave the cupcakes in the tin for 5 minutes, then gently lift them out on to a wire rack (I find a fork helpful for this) and leave to cool.

For the icing, mix the icing sugar and water with a tiny dab of the Grape Violet food colouring, adding the colour a speck at a time until you have a nice pale lavender shade.

Ice each cake with 2 teaspoons of icing, either making a neat circle in the middle, or flooding the cake to the edges (easier if you aren't a neat icer, which I am not).

Place a lavender sprig in the middle of each cake as you go, and let the icing set completely before serving.

The cakes will keep well in an airtight container in a cool room for 2–3 days.

FOR GLUTEN-FREE: use gluten-free self-raising flour and add 40ml milk.

ROSE & PISTACHIO CUPCAKES

These taste as good as they look: a variation on the blackberry pistachio cake in *The Quick Roasting Tin*, these cupcakes are very lightly flavoured with rose water. Go gently, as it can be a strong flavouring – you want a very light hint of rose here.

Makes: 12
Prep: 10 minutes
Cook: 20 minutes

100g shelled pistachios
115g softened unsalted butter
115g caster sugar
2 medium free-range eggs
30g gluten-free plain flour
   or ordinary plain flour if not
   making gluten-free)
1 teaspoon baking powder
40ml milk
½ teaspoon rose water

ICING
200g icing sugar
30ml water
A smudge of green food colouring
Dried rose petals
   or gluten-free wafer roses,
   to decorate

Preheat the oven to 160°C fan/180°C/gas 4. Blitz the pistachios in a food processor, spice grinder or Nutribullet until very finely ground (but don't over-blitz, or they'll get oily).

Beat the butter and caster sugar together until light and fluffy, then whisk in the eggs, one at a time.

Mix through the ground pistachios, flour, baking powder, milk and rose water, then divide the mixture equally between 12 paper cases in a cupcake tin – this will be about 2 heaped teaspoons per case.

Transfer the cakes to the oven and bake for 20 minutes, until well risen, golden brown and a skewer inserted into the middle comes out clean.

Cool on a wire rack, and meanwhile, mix your icing sugar and water together with a smudge of food colouring until you have a pale pistachio green. (I recommend Sugarflair Kiwi, but if you are using bottles, use a tiny bit of green and yellow.) Ice the cooled cakes and decorate with dried rose petals or wafer roses as preferred.

These will keep in an airtight container for 2–3 days.

BLACK FOREST CUPCAKES

A very manageable version of the magnificent Black Forest gateaux you find in cake shops in Germany – sometimes a gal just needs chocolate, cream and cherries all together in cake form. I prefer mascarpone to whipped cream, so have included it here, but by all means substitute lightly whipped double cream if you wish. Sour cherries will give you that classic flavour in the topping.

Makes: 12
Prep: 10 minutes
Cook: 12–15 minutes

115g softened unsalted butter
115g caster sugar
   (golden if preferred)
2 medium free-range eggs
90g self-raising flour
25g cocoa powder
1 teaspoon baking powder
40ml milk

ICING
100g defrosted frozen
   or jarred pitted morello cherries
   (sour cherries are best)
2 teaspoons caster sugar
100g mascarpone, beaten
12 fresh cherries, to decorate
   (optional)

Preheat the oven to 160°C fan/180°C/gas 4. Whisk the butter and sugar together until pale and fluffy, then beat in the eggs one at a time.

Gently fold in the flour, cocoa powder and baking powder along with the milk, taking care not to overmix. Divide the batter equally between 12 paper cases in a cupcake or muffin tin.

Transfer the cakes to the oven and bake for 12–15 minutes, until firm to the touch and a skewer inserted comes out clean.

Leave the cupcakes in the tin for 5 minutes, then gently lift them out on to a wire rack (I find a fork helpful for this) and leave to cool completely.

For the icing, halve the cherries and toss with the caster sugar. Stir the cherries through the beaten mascarpone very gently – you want to retain a pink and white swirl of colour rather than making a pink icing (though this is not the end of the world).

Place a heaped teaspoon of the mascarpone and cherry mix on each cake, top with a fresh cherry and serve immediately.

As you'll have to eat the iced cakes the day you assemble them, you can make the cakes in advance and keep them un-iced in an airtight container in a cool room for 2–3 days. Keep the mascarpone and cherry mix in the fridge (it will become pinker) and ice as you go.

ROSEMARY LEMON CURD CUPCAKES

These are gorgeous, grown-up cupcakes – rosemary works beautifully in the sponge against the sharp lemon curd. By all means use your own home-made – I am a little lazy and tend to use good bought instead.

Makes: 12
Prep: 10 minutes
Cook: 15 minutes

115g softened unsalted butter
115g caster sugar
2 medium free-range eggs
115g self-raising flour
1 teaspoon baking powder
1 teaspoon chopped fresh
  rosemary
20ml milk
12 heaped teaspoons lemon curd
12 rosemary tips

Preheat the oven to 160°C fan/180°C/gas 4. Whisk the butter and sugar together until pale and fluffy, then beat in the eggs one at a time.

Gently fold in the self-raising flour and baking powder along with the chopped rosemary and the milk, taking care not to overmix. Divide the batter equally between 12 paper cases in a cupcake or muffin tin.

Transfer the cakes to the oven and bake for 15 minutes, until firm to the touch and a skewer inserted comes out clean.

Leave the cupcakes in the tin for 5 minutes, then gently lift them out on to a wire rack (I find a fork helpful for this) and leave to cool.

Spread a neat circle of lemon curd on top of each cake, and top with a rosemary tip.

The cakes will keep well in an airtight container un-iced in a cool room for 2–3 days – once you put the lemon curd on, you'll need to store any spare cakes in the fridge.

FOR GLUTEN-FREE: these cakes work so beautifully with gluten-free flour (I use the Freee self-raising blend from Doves Farm) that I often make it with that instead of ordinary self-raising flour – texturally, it works really well with the flavour of the rosemary. Just increase the amount of milk to 40ml rather than 20ml, as the gluten-free mix is more absorbent.

PINEAPPLE & COCONUT CUPCAKES

A variation on two of my favourite desserts, pineapple upside-down cake and coconut macaroons. These lovely tropical cupcakes are dusted with just the barest hint of cinnamon – these are probably the most addictive in the chapter.

Makes: 12
Prep: 10 minutes
Cook: 15–20 minutes

115g softened unsalted butter
115g caster sugar
2 medium free-range eggs
90g unsweetened desiccated
   coconut
30g gluten-free plain flour
   (or ordinary plain flour, if not
   making gluten-free)
1 teaspoon baking powder
150g pineapple chunks, drained
A tiny pinch of ground cinnamon,
   to dust

Preheat the oven to 160°C fan/180°C/gas 4. Beat the butter and caster sugar together until light and fluffy, then whisk in the eggs, one at a time.

Mix in the desiccated coconut, flour and baking powder, then divide the mixture equally between paper cases in a 12-hole cupcake tin – this will be about 2 heaped teaspoons per case.

Arrange a few chunks of pineapple on top of each cake (eat any remaining pineapple) and dust the tops with a tiny pinch of cinnamon.

Transfer the cakes to the oven and bake for 15–20 minutes, until firm, golden brown, well risen and a skewer inserted into the middle comes out clean.

Cool on a wire rack and serve warm or at room temperature. You can keep these in the fridge in an airtight container for 2 days.

RASPBERRY BAKEWELL CUPCAKES

I almost called these 'Emergency Bakewell Cupcakes', for those moments when you want a Bakewell tart, and you want it 5 minutes ago. These quick cupcakes might just take the edge off – an easy frangipane filling topped with crisp flaked almonds, with a hidden raspberry jam centre.

Makes: 12
Prep: 10 minutes
Cook: 15 minutes

115g softened unsalted butter
115g caster sugar
2 medium free-range eggs
100g ground almonds
30g gluten-free plain flour
   (or ordinary plain flour,
   if not making gluten-free)
1 teaspoon baking powder
6 heaped teaspoons
   raspberry jam
A handful of flaked almonds

Preheat the oven to 160°C fan/180°C/gas 4. Whisk the butter and sugar together until pale and fluffy, then beat in the eggs one at a time.

Gently fold in the ground almonds, flour and baking powder, taking care not to overmix. Put a heaped teaspoon of batter into each paper case in a 12-hole cupcake or muffin tin and top each with half a teaspoon of jam before dividing the remaining batter equally between the cases.

Scatter the flaked almonds over the top of each cake, then transfer the cakes to the oven and bake for 15 minutes, until firm to the touch and a skewer inserted comes out clean.

Leave the cupcakes in the tin for 5 minutes, then gently lift them out on to a wire rack (I find a fork helpful for this) and leave to cool before serving warm or at room temperature.

The cakes will keep well in an airtight container in a cool room for 2–3 days.

DOUGH

RAINBOW ICED BUNS

CHOCOLATE, ALMOND & RAISIN
JUMBLE BREAD

CARDAMOM & CINNAMON KNOTS

CARAMEL APPLE CHELSEA BUNS

STUFFED ROSEMARY & ROASTED GARLIC
DOUGH BALLS

CAMEMBERT DIPPING WHEEL

PARMESAN & PARMA HAM BUNS

SPICED FOCACCIA WITH
ROASTED BUTTERNUT SQUASH
(VEGAN)

DOUGH

In this chapter, I give you my simplest and favourite sweet dough recipe, lightly enriched with butter, milk and egg so the finished product has the fluffy softness of a good iced bun. It's much easier to work with than a fully enriched brioche dough, so if you aren't using a mixer with a dough hook, you'll be able to get it into a kneadable shape within a few minutes. I've included variations overleaf for vegan sweet and savoury doughs. For the perfect, fluffy bun, here are a few things to bear in mind:

FLOUR

For all the recipes in this chapter, you'll need strong white bread flour. However, not all strong white bread flours are the same: even if you buy two bags of the same brand, the absorbency of the flour will vary – more so if you've got 'extra strong' white bread flour. So that brings us on to:

LIQUID

Go slowly – pour the liquid into your flour a bit at a time, and mix with a wooden spoon as you go. As some flours will be more absorbent, and some less, you may need a fraction more or less liquid – I've been known to get my hand in to mix for the last couple of liquid additions, to check the texture and consistency.

You're looking for a slightly sticky rather than a dry dough, so resist the temptation to add more flour – it's the moisture content that will give you that light, airy texture at the end.

In the vegan version, I use olive oil and oat milk or water rather than butter and ordinary milk – but you could of course experiment with other oils, like coconut, and your preferred vegan milks.

YEAST

Use fast action or easy bake, as you can add it directly to the flour. I like to buy these in little tins that you can keep in the fridge, rather than in sachets (more packaging, and you need 4g yeast for all the recipes in this chapter rather than the 7g in each sachet).

SUGAR

There's just 30g of sugar in the sweet bun recipes, as you're adding sweetness through the toppings or fillings. I've left a teaspoon of sugar in the savoury version to help the yeast along.

If cooking for a diabetic, replace the sugar in the sweet bun recipes with half the weight of xylitol: so 15g of xylitol rather than 30g of sugar, and omit the sugar altogether for the savoury dough.

SALT

I love salt, but yeast does not. As long as you mix the flour and yeast together before adding the salt (so it doesn't touch the yeast directly to start with), you'll be fine – I like to include a pinch even in the sweet dough recipes to improve the flavour.

KNEADING VS DOUGH HOOKS VS BREAD MACHINES

All the doughs below are designed to be kneadable by hand – they may start out sticky, but try to resist the temptation to add more flour – a tiny bit on the work surface and on your hands is fine, but the dough should come together nicely within a couple of minutes of kneading, and after 7–10 minutes be springy, smooth and feel slightly, but not alarmingly, alive.

If you have a dough hook and a freestanding mixer, you can stick everything in and mix it in there, and if you have a bread machine with a kneading programme, follow the instructions for what order to put in the liquid, flour and any additional flavourings.

I'm by no means a purist and will use the freestanding mixer nine times out of ten, but you will get the best feel for how the dough is behaving if you knead by hand.

ALL-PURPOSE SWEET DOUGH

325g strong white bread flour

4g fast action/easy bake dried yeast

30g caster sugar

A pinch of sea salt

40g unsalted butter

150ml milk

1 medium free-range egg

ALL-PURPOSE VEGAN SWEET DOUGH

325g strong white bread flour

4g fast action/easy bake dried yeast

30g caster sugar

A pinch of sea salt

50ml olive oil

170ml full-fat oat milk

ALL-PURPOSE SAVOURY DOUGH (ALSO VEGAN)

325g strong white bread flour

4g fast action/ easy bake dried yeast

1 teaspoon sugar

1 teaspoon sea salt flakes

70ml olive oil

150ml water

FOR DIABETICS

Replace the sugar in the sweet dough recipes above with half the weight of xylitol, so 15g xylitol instead of 30g sugar.

Omit the sugar from the savoury dough.

Please see page 225 for the nutritional information for the diabetic versions of the buns in this chapter.

METHOD
FOR ALL THREE DOUGHS

Measure the flour, fast action dried yeast and sugar into a large bowl, stir, then add the salt. If you have any small-volume flavouring ingredients to add to the dough – e.g. finely chopped rosemary, ground cardamom – add them now.

For the all-purpose sweet dough, put the butter and milk into a small saucepan and heat gently until the butter has just melted. Take the mixture off the heat and let it cool until tepid to the touch. (You can pour the milk and melted butter into a cold bowl to speed this up.) Whisk in the egg.

For either of the vegan doughs, measure the oil and milk or oil and water into a jug – don't worry about whisking it.

Pour the liquid ingredients into the flour mixture, stirring slowly with a wooden spoon until everything just comes together as a slightly sticky dough.

Now you have three choices: with lightly floured hands, you can knead the dough for 10 minutes and watch it go from sticky and recalcitrant (1–3 minutes) to nicely workable (3–5 minutes) to wonderfully smooth, silky and springy (5–10 minutes). Try not to add any more flour between minutes 1 and 3 – I promise it will come together with a bit of patience, albeit with a sticky work surface and hands to start with.

The other option is to stick the dough into a stand mixer, and knead with a dough hook on a medium setting for 7–10 minutes, until smooth and springy. Your final option is to use the kneading programme on a bread machine, according to the manufacturer's instructions.

Once you have a nicely kneaded dough (smooth, springy, elastic – if you prod it with your fingertip, the indentation should spring back), you can carefully fold through any larger additional ingredients – chopped nuts, chocolate chips, almonds, etc.

Shape the dough into a round, place in a large, lightly oiled bowl, cover with a damp tea towel or clingfilm, then leave to rise at room temperature for 1–2 hours, until doubled in size. This is going to depend on how warm your room is – a slow prove is going to give you better results than sticking it in the airing cupboard, so ideally, leave it in a cool room, and you won't risk over-proving, which can make it collapse later.

Once the dough has doubled in size, punch it down (satisfying), then follow your chosen recipe for shaping and baking.

If you have time, or perhaps want the buns for breakfast on a Sunday morning and are making the dough on a Saturday evening, you can start proving at room temperature for around half an hour, before transferring the covered bowl of dough to the fridge overnight for a cold prove. This will improve the flavour, as it allows the yeast to work slowly – just get it back to room temperature for 30 minutes before knocking back and shaping. It will take a little longer to rise after shaping.

To test if your buns are cooked, flip one over and give it a tap – it should sound hollow. Alternately, sacrifice one by cutting it open to check.

For further reading and dough troubleshooting: see *Crumb* by Ruby Tandoh.

RAINBOW ICED BUNS

My – and perhaps your – first bun love was pink or white iced buns from the supermarket. Looked like a bun, magically tasted like air and sugar, and the all-important choice – white or pink? My younger sister was convinced the pink ones were strawberry flavoured, but she's come round to realising they were just sugar-flavoured – as are these beauties below. Please don't worry if your buns aren't as regular-shaped as the supermarket kind – they will taste just as good.

Makes: 8 buns
Prep: 15 minutes
           + 2 hours rising
Cook: 15 minutes

BUNS
1 x quantity all-purpose
   sweet dough
   or vegan sweet dough
   (see page 179)

ICING
200g icing sugar
30ml water
A few drops of food colouring

Follow the method on page 180 until your dough has proved.

Knock back the proved dough, then divide it into 8 equal pieces – you can weigh these out if you want to be super-precise, but I usually do them by eye.

Roll each piece into an even sausage around 10cm long, and place them in rows on a lined baking tray about 2cm apart – you want them to lightly touch as they rise.

Leave the buns to prove for 20–30 minutes, until one and a half times their original size, then preheat the oven to 180°C fan/200°C/gas 6.

Transfer the buns to the oven and bake on a low shelf for 15 minutes, until well risen and golden brown on top. Place on a wire rack to cool, and gently tear or cut the buns apart.

Mix the icing sugar with the water a little at a time to form a thick icing, and divide between two bowls. Add a few drops or dabs of pink food colouring to one bowl and mix to your preferred shade.

Use a tablespoon to carefully ice the cooled buns, and serve when the icing has set.

CHOCOLATE, ALMOND & RAISIN JUMBLE BREAD

My two favourite buns from the Danish bakery Ole & Steen are the kløben bun, with almonds and raisins, and the higgledy-piggledy chocolate chip bun. I can never decide between them, so I order both, and eat them one after the other – even though each is about the size of my head. These jumbled-up chocolate chip, almond and raisin buns are my homage to both.

Makes:	8 buns
Prep:	20 minutes
	+ 2 hours rising
Cook:	20–25 minutes

BUNS
1 unwaxed orange, zest only
1 x quantity all-purpose sweet
  dough or vegan sweet dough
  (see page 179)

FILLING
50g raisins
50g toasted flaked almonds
50g chopped dark chocolate
  (I like 70% cocoa solids; check
  the label for vegan if needed)

TO FINISH
1 medium free-range egg, lightly
  beaten, or oat milk, for brushing

FOR DIABETICS: use the xylitol version of the sweet bun dough (see page 179), and make sure your chocolate is diabetic-friendly – good diabetic dark chocolate is available online.

Stir the orange zest with the other dough ingredients, then follow the method on page 180 until you've kneaded your dough for about 10 minutes.

Flatten the dough into a large rectangle and tip the raisins, flaked almonds and dark chocolate into the middle, then roll the dough up like a Swiss roll – this ensures an even distribution.

Curl the dough back up into a ball, and gently knead for a further minute to fully incorporate the nuts, raisins and chocolate – they'll try to run away, but don't worry, just squash any escapees back into the dough.

Roll the dough into a ball, transfer to a lightly oiled bowl, then cover with clingfilm or a damp tea towel and leave to rise for 1–2 hours at room temperature, until doubled in size.

Once the dough has proved, punch it back down, then divide it into 8 equal pieces. You can shape these as you wish, but I like to take each eighth, twist it tightly as if making a helter-skelter or candy cane, then loop the twist into a circle, and press the ends to join – a bit like a twisty doughnut. Place each shape on a lined baking tray and leave to rise for 20–30 minutes, until one and a half times their original size.

Once the buns have risen, preheat the oven to 160°C fan/180°C/gas 4. Very gently brush the tops of the buns with the beaten egg or oat milk, then transfer to the oven and bake for 20–25 minutes, until well risen, golden brown and cooked through. Cool briefly on a wire rack and serve warm.

CARDAMOM & CINNAMON KNOTS

Cardamom is my favourite spice, and these are subsequently my favourite buns – I cannot pass a bakery selling them without buying at least two (one for now, one for later). These are perfect warm with a cup of coffee: if they don't all get eaten in one go, warm them through before serving the next day, or stash a few in a bag in the freezer for later bun-emergencies.

Makes:	13–16 mini buns
Prep:	30 minutes
	+ 2 hours proving
Cook:	15 minutes

BUNS

3 cardamom pods, seeds ground,
   outer pods discarded
1 x quantity all-purpose sweet
   dough or vegan sweet dough
   (see page 179)

FILLING

60g softened unsalted butter
   or vegan plant-based spread,
   cubed (at room temperature)
4 cardamom pods, seeds ground,
   outer pods discarded
½ teaspoon cinnamon
60g soft light brown sugar

TO FINISH

1 medium free-range egg, beaten,
   or oat milk, for brushing

FOR DIABETICS: use the xylitol version of the sweet bun dough (see page 179), and replace the sugar in the filling with 60g mashed dates.

Stir the ground cardamom in with the dough, and continue with the method on page 180 until the dough has proved.

For the filling, mix the butter or plant-based spread, ground cardamom, cinnamon and sugar together.

Knock back the dough, then roll it out on a clean, lightly flour-dusted surface into a rectangle, approx. 30cm x 20cm.

Spread the filling all over the surface of the dough, then fold it in half lengthways (to leave you with a 30cm x 10cm thicker rectangle).

Cut the dough into 13–16 equal-sized strips, then tie each strip into a double knot. Place on a large lined baking sheet – don't worry that they won't all look exactly the same, they're home-style buns.

Leave the knots at room temperature for 20–30 minutes, until about one and a half times their original size, then preheat the oven to 180°C fan/200°C/gas 6.

Brush the knots with the beaten egg or a little oat milk – very gently, so as not to squash the dough – then transfer to the oven and bake for 15 minutes, until golden brown and cooked through. (Check them after 13 minutes if your oven runs hot.) Let the buns cool for 5 minutes or so on a wire rack before tucking in.

CARAMEL APPLE CHELSEA BUNS

These are a lovely autumnal treat – perfect to serve around Bonfire Night. The trick to getting nice uniform buns is to use a roasting tin to help shape them into neat squares as they rise – they can't escape as they would on an ordinary baking tray. Serve iced or un-iced, as you wish.

Makes: 12–15 buns
Prep: 30 minutes
        + 2 hours proving
Cook: 20 minutes

BUNS

1 teaspoon ground cinnamon
1 x quantity all-purpose sweet
    dough (see page 179)

FILLING

1 large apple (about 180g),
    finely chopped
60g unsalted butter
150g tinned caramel
½ teaspoon ground cinnamon
40g hazelnuts, toasted
    and chopped
1 medium free-range egg, beaten,
    for brushing
2 teaspoons demerara sugar

You will need a lined approx. 25cm round roasting tin, so the buns can stick together as they rise.

Stir the ground cinnamon in with the flour, and continue with the method on page 180 until your dough has proved.

For the filling, tip the chopped apple, butter, caramel and cinnamon into a saucepan, and stir over a medium to low heat for 5 minutes, until the apples have just softened. Stir in the toasted chopped hazelnuts and leave to cool.

Once the dough has proved, knock it back, then roll it out on a clean surface into a large square, approx. 30cm x 30cm. Spread the filling all over the dough, leaving a 2.5cm border around the edges. Roll the dough up tightly – it will stretch to almost double its length as you do this, that's fine. Cut the dough into 2.5cm slices, and carefully transfer them to a lined roasting tin, placing them neatly as you go.

Leave the buns to rise for 25–30 minutes, until about one and a half times their original size, then preheat the oven to 180°C fan/200°C/gas 6.

Brush the tops of the buns with the beaten egg (very gently, so as not to squash the dough), scatter with the demerara sugar, then transfer to the oven and bake for 20 minutes, until golden brown and cooked through. Let the buns cool for 10 minutes or so on a wire rack, then carefully cut them apart with a knife and serve. You can ice the finished buns with a drizzle of glacé icing using the recipe on page 26.

STUFFED ROSEMARY & ROASTED GARLIC DOUGH BALLS

During the first lockdown, my mother and I made the Camembert dipping wheel on the following page after going down a YouTube recipe video spiral. It was a tremendous success, and we wanted to make it for my sister on her first socially distanced visit – before realising that a tear-and-share bread wasn't particularly in keeping with staying two metres apart. So I adapted the recipe into these dough balls (which I absolutely did not throw across the room for her to catch) – they feel easy enough to knock out on a Friday evening at home – and you can save the celebratory centrepiece for a party.

Makes: 16
Prep: 20 minutes
+ 2 hours proving
Cook: 15 minutes, +15–20
minutes for the garlic

DOUGH
1 teaspoon chopped
fresh rosemary
1 x quantity all-purpose
savoury dough (see page 179)

FILLING
2 cloves of garlic, unpeeled
½ tablespoon olive oil
130g Camembert, mozzarella
or plant-based cheese,
cut into 16 pieces

TO FINISH
A pinch of sea salt flakes

FOR DIABETICS: omit the sugar from the savoury dough recipe.

TO VEGANISE: use vegan Camembert or mozzarella.

Stir the chopped rosemary with the flour, and continue with the method on page 180 until your dough has proved.

While the dough is proving, roast the garlic cloves in their skins with the olive oil for 15–20 minutes at 180°C fan/200°C/gas 6, then leave to cool. Squeeze the garlic out of their skins, mash with the back of a fork, then mix with the pieces of cheese.

Once the dough has proved, knock it back, then divide into 16 equal pieces. Flatten each piece into a round in your hand, just smaller than palm-size, and place a piece of cheese in the middle. Fold the dough around the cheese, then pinch and twist tightly to close (you don't want any gaps, or the cheese will escape).

Transfer to a lined baking sheet, pinched side down, and continue with the rest of the dough.

Let the dough balls rise for 20–30 minutes at room temperature, then preheat the oven to 180°C fan/200°C/gas 6 again.

Scatter the tops of the dough balls with a pinch of sea salt, and bake for 15 minutes, until well risen and golden brown. Serve hot.

CAMEMBERT DIPPING WHEEL

This is a wonderful, indulgent treat to serve with drinks – though we've been known to make and eat it for a savoury brunch too. It's a little hard to describe in words how to shape it, so you can head to my website for a video if you like (see page 236).

Serves: 4
Prep: 30 minutes
+ 2 hours rising
Cook: 20 minutes

DOUGH
A handful of sage leaves, chopped
1 teaspoon chopped
fresh rosemary
1 x quantity all-purpose savoury
dough (see page 179)

TOPPING
1 x 250g Camembert
(vegetarian if needed)
A handful of small sage leaves
A pinch of sea salt flakes
1 clove of garlic, peeled
and thickly sliced
Extra virgin olive oil, to drizzle

FOR DIABETICS: omit the sugar from the savoury dough recipe.

TO VEGANISE: use vegan Camembert.

Stir the chopped sage and rosemary with the flour, then follow the method on page 180 until you've kneaded your dough for about 10 minutes.

Roll the dough into a ball, transfer to a lightly oiled bowl, then cover and leave to rise for 1–2 hours at room temperature, until doubled in size.

Once the dough has proved, punch it back down, then place it on a large, lined baking sheet. Flatten it, and make a small hole in the middle before rolling it out to the size of a dinner plate, widening the gap in the middle to the size of the cheese.

Place the unwrapped whole Camembert in the gap, then, using a sharp knife, cut 2.5cm 'spokes' all around – as if creating a child's illustration of the sun – being careful not to cut all the way to the middle (you'll want a 1cm circle of dough around the Camembert before the spokes start).

Twist each spoke tightly with a couple of sage leaves in each, and arrange into a curved shape as opposite. Scatter the dough and cheese with the remaining sage leaves and sea salt. Make a few indentations in the Camembert with a sharp knife, and stick the garlic in.

Leave the wheel to rise for 20–30 minutes, then preheat the oven to 180°C fan/200°C/gas 6.

Drizzle the wheel with a little olive oil, then transfer to the oven and bake for 20 minutes, until the spokes are golden brown and the cheese has melted. Serve hot.

PARMESAN & PARMA HAM BUNS

These light, savoury buns are wonderful with soup or a cheeseboard. I like to make a batch and stash most of them in the freezer – they defrost and warm up really quickly in the oven for a last-minute lunch or addition to home-made soup.

Makes: 16 buns
Prep: 15 minutes
            + 1–2 hours rising
Cook: 15 minutes

BUNS
1 x quantity all-purpose savoury
   dough (see page 179)

FILLING
72g packet Parma ham,
   roughly chopped
   into small shreds
20g Parmesan, finely grated
A handful of oregano leaves,
   chopped

TOPPING
10g grated Parmesan

Follow the method on page 180 until you've kneaded your dough for about 10 minutes. Flatten the dough out into a large rectangle, tip the Parma ham, Parmesan and oregano evenly over the top, then roll the dough up like a Swiss roll – this ensures an even distribution.

Curl the dough back up into a ball, and gently knead for a further minute to fully incorporate the filling – bits of herb and Parmesan may fall out, but you can press them back into the dough.

Roll the dough into a ball, transfer to a lightly oiled bowl, then cover with clingfilm or a damp tea towel and leave to rise for 1–2 hours at room temperature, until doubled in size.

Once the dough has proved, punch it back down, then divide it into 16 equal pieces. Pinch and twist each piece to create a taut, round surface on the other side – this will make sure they look like nice rounds when they bake. Transfer to a lined baking sheet, pinched side down, and leave to rise for 20–30 minutes, or until one and a half times their original size.

Preheat the oven to 180°C fan/200°C/gas 6. Evenly scatter the grated Parmesan over the buns and bake for 15 minutes, until well risen, golden brown and cooked through.

Transfer to a wire rack to cool briefly before eating.

FOR DIABETICS: omit the sugar from the savoury dough recipe.

SPICED FOCACCIA
WITH ROASTED BUTTERNUT SQUASH

I love the sense of achievement with knocking out a focaccia – and this one, topped with roasted butternut squash, is almost a meal in itself. You could just as easily use cherry tomatoes, or finely sliced red onion – and if you can't find dukkah, try za'atar, which should be available in the supermarket spice aisle.

Serves: 6
Prep: 25 minutes
+ 2 hours proving
Cook: 30–35 minutes,
+ 30 minutes
for the squash

DOUGH
2 tablespoons dukkah
or za'atar
1 x quantity all-purpose
savoury dough (see page 179)

TOPPING
400g butternut squash,
cut into 1.5cm cubes
1 tablespoon olive oil, plus extra
for drizzling
A handful of fresh sage,
roughly torn
2 teaspoons sea salt flakes
1 tablespoon dukkah

I like to make the focaccia in a lined 24cm x 17cm roasting tin, so it grows in a neat rectangle – it helps to keep the topping in place too.

Stir the dukkah or za'atar with the flour, and continue with the method on page 180 until your dough has proved.

While the dough is proving, roast the cubed butternut squash with the olive oil, sage and 1 teaspoon of sea salt for 30 minutes at 180°C fan/200°C/gas 6, then leave to cool.

Once the dough has proved, punch it down and roll it into a rectangle, roughly the same size as your lined roasting tin.

Scatter the dough with the roasted butternut squash, dukkah and remaining teaspoon of sea salt, pressing the ingredients deep into the dough with your fingers. Cover and leave to rise for 20–30 minutes, until doubled in size.

Preheat the oven to 180°C fan/200°C/gas 6 again. Drizzle the focaccia generously with olive oil and bake for 30–35 minutes, until well risen, browned and firm to the touch. Cool on a wire rack, then cut into fingers and serve.

HIGH DAYS
& HOLIDAYS
AROUND THE WORLD

ZOE'S GRANNY'S FRUIT CAKE

CHOCOLATE, CLEMENTINE
& STEM GINGER PUDDINGS

ICED & SPICED GINGERBREAD

MARZIPAN STOLLEN

DATE & WALNUT RUGELACH

TARTA DE SANTIAGO

(GLUTEN-FREE)

COCONUT BURFI

(GLUTEN-FREE)

HIGH DAYS & HOLIDAYS AROUND THE WORLD

The idea for this chapter comes from Rachel, my publisher, and she was so right to suggest it: sharing baked goods with friends and family on special holidays is a universal pleasure. And so alongside a classic fruit cake – perfect for everything from Christmas to weddings to christenings – you'll find German marzipan stollen (see page 210), Jewish date and walnut rugelach (see page 214), Spanish almond cake (see page 216) and my favourite Indian sweet, coconut burfi (see page 218) – a random selection, yes, but some of my favourite sweet things to eat from around the world.

Perhaps the nicest thing about holiday baking is the tradition behind it, and the stories that families and friends accumulate around certain dishes. The fruit cake recipe in this chapter (see page 204) comes from my friend Zoe's granny, and has built up cult status in Zoe's family and beyond: it's impossible to try the cake and not ask for the recipe, and I can't count the number of times I have passed it on. Zoe recounts that after her granny died, her grandpa attempted to make the cake from memory. 'It was touted as an absolute disaster,' she says – 'he'd somehow separated all the fats and they'd floated to the top of the cake in a layer.' He was (lovingly) mocked by the family. (I can promise that if you follow the written recipe, you'll have no such problem.) When her granny made the cake during the war, she'd use anything to hand, including dried egg – but more recently, Zoe's mum has found that you get a wonderful result from gluten-free flour. If there's a recipe that will become a firm family favourite from this book, I have no doubts that it'll be this one. (With the date and walnut rugelach a close second. I'm slightly addicted and can't stop making them.)

ZOE'S GRANNY'S FRUIT CAKE

The recipe for this fruit cake was given to me by my university friend Zoe, who served it at a Christmas party at her flat in Edinburgh. Made by her mother, it was hands down the nicest fruit cake I've ever tried, and I've been making it for the last fifteen years on request for friends' weddings, as Christmas gifts and for birthdays, with the recipe itself passed on almost as many times. I can claim no credit: Zoe's granny was on to a winner with this wartime recipe. It's wonderfully forgiving, and I include her original notes and suggestions for substitutions below.

Serves: a lot
Prep: 30 minutes
Cook: 2½–3 hours

350g softened unsalted butter
350g soft dark brown sugar
1 teaspoon vanilla extract
1 teaspoon almond extract
1 lemon, zest and juice
1 tablespoon black treacle (optional)
1 tablespoon marmalade (optional)
350g plain flour
55g ground almonds
1 small teaspoon salt

1 teaspoon mixed spice
1 teaspoon ground cinnamon
½ teaspoon ground nutmeg
7 medium free-range eggs
450g sultanas
450g currants
225g raisins
225g glacé cherries
115g chopped almonds

Preheat the oven to 115°C fan/135°C/gas 1. Cream the butter, sugar, extracts and the lemon zest and juice, along with the treacle and marmalade, if using.

In a separate bowl, mix the flour and ground almonds with the salt and spices.

Add the eggs to the creamed mixture – one at a time with tablespoons of the flour mix to prevent it from curdling. Beat well.

Fold in the rest of the flour mix and the fruit and nuts, then transfer to a lined cake tin (see notes below) and bake in the oven for 2½– 3 hours, covering with tinfoil if it starts getting too dark on top.

ZOE'S GRANNY'S NOTES: We made cakes after the war with all sorts of proportions. I usually put in a tablespoon of coffee with a spot of milk. The recipe makes my big 10-inch (25cm) cake tin, or one 8-inch (20cm) and one 7-inch (18cm). I butter the tin and flour it, and put a layer of foil outside, standing higher than the tin. I don't worry too much about the actual proportions of fruit, just make sure they are the correct total – I've included dried apricots, dates, prunes, etc. I often use walnuts instead because they're cheaper. Good luck!

MINI'S NOTES: Very little can go wrong with this cake, and I always feed it with brandy for a good month or two before it's to be eaten, whether for Christmas, Easter or a friend's wedding. To do this, let the cake cool down completely, then use a skewer to make 8–10 small holes in the top. Spoon over a few tablespoons of brandy/amaretto, then wrap in baking parchment and tinfoil, and keep in an airtight container. Continue to feed once a week, turning the cake over each time. You can marzipan and ice the cake a few days before you need it, or decorate it with candied fruit and whole blanched almonds or mixed nuts, with apricot jam (melted and sieved) brushed over to glaze.

CHOCOLATE, CLEMENTINE
& STEM GINGER PUDDINGS

These are mini Christmas puddings for people who inexplicably don't like dried fruit (I'm particularly addressing my sister here). These chocolate, orange and ginger offerings are a lovely festive dessert, reminiscent of the best sort of school pudding. Serve with crème fraîche or hot custard.

Makes: 6
Prep: 15 minutes
Cook: 25–30 minutes

4 pieces of stem ginger,
    finely chopped
115g softened unsalted butter
115g soft light brown sugar
2 medium free-range eggs
2 clementines, zest and juice
85g plain flour
30g cocoa powder
1 teaspoon baking powder
6 squares dark chocolate
    (70% cocoa solids)
crème fraîche or custard
    and clementine slices, to serve

Preheat the oven to 160°C fan/180°C/gas 4, and butter 6 dariole moulds. Set half the chopped stem ginger to one side, and divide the rest equally between the moulds. Whisk the butter and sugar together until smooth, then beat in the eggs one at a time, along with the clementine zest and juice and the rest of the chopped stem ginger.

Gently fold in the plain flour, cocoa powder and baking powder, taking care not to overmix.

Fill each dariole mould halfway with the batter, place a square of chocolate in the middle, then carry on filling the moulds.

Place the moulds in a medium-sized, deep roasting tin, and carefully pour in boiling water to come halfway up the sides of the moulds. Cover the tin tightly with tinfoil, then gently transfer to the oven and cook for 25–30 minutes.

Remove the moulds from the water with tongs, gently run a knife around the sides of each pudding, and invert on to a plate. Serve hot, with crème fraîche or custard and clementine slices.

ICED & SPICED GINGERBREAD

Despite the very gingery theme of this book, these mini loaves with their gilded icing are just too nice not to include in a holiday baking chapter. Perfect as a hostess gift or for a special winter afternoon tea at home.

Makes: 8
Prep: 10 minutes
Cook: 25 minutes

170ml olive oil
170ml date syrup
5cm fresh ginger, finely grated
3 medium free-range eggs
70g ground almonds
100g self-raising flour
1 teaspoon baking powder
1 teaspoon ground ginger
A grating of fresh nutmeg
½ teaspoon ground cinnamon

TOPPING
200g icing sugar
30ml lemon juice
A handful of chopped
   crystallised ginger
Edible gold spray (optional)

Preheat the oven to 160°C fan/180°C/gas 4. Whisk the olive oil, date syrup and grated ginger together; when smoothly incorporated, beat in the eggs one at a time.

Gently fold in the ground almonds, self-raising flour, baking powder, ground ginger, nutmeg and cinnamon, taking care not to overmix.

Spoon the batter into 8 lined mini-loaf tins (you could also use a muffin tin), then transfer to the oven and bake for 25 minutes, until firm to the touch and a skewer inserted comes out clean.

Let the loaves cool on a wire rack. Once cold, mix the icing sugar with the lemon juice and ice the cakes, scattering over the crystallised ginger as opposite.

Once the icing has set, you can spritz gently with edible gold spray. These will keep well in an airtight container for 2–3 days.

FOR GLUTEN-FREE: replace the self-raising flour with gluten-free self-raising flour.

MARZIPAN STOLLEN

German Christmas food is exactly what I want to eat and drink when December hits – lebkuchen, glühwein, gingerbread houses – and of course, stollen. This is surprisingly easy to make (admittedly, if you have a dough hook attachment), and very much worth it – the house will smell wonderful as it cooks, too.

Serves:	8–10
Prep:	45 minutes
	+ 3 hours rising
Cook:	25–30 minutes

110ml milk
350g plain flour
5g fast action/easy bake
   dried yeast
250g mixed dried fruit
   (without mixed peel)
100ml brandy
40g caster sugar
A pinch of sea salt
½ teaspoon ground cinnamon
½ teaspoon grated nutmeg
1 orange, zest only
1 lemon, zest only
1 medium free-range egg, beaten
110g unsalted butter, melted
150g marzipan
3 tablespoons melted butter
   + icing sugar, to serve

Heat the milk in a saucepan until just barely warm to the touch (if it gets hotter than that, let it cool back to tepid). Stir in 50g of the flour and the yeast, and leave to pre-ferment for 30 minutes, after which it will look thick and bubbly.

Meanwhile, stir the dried fruit with the brandy, and set aside.

Tip the remaining flour, sugar, salt, cinnamon, nutmeg and citrus zest into a large bowl, and set aside.

Once the pre-ferment is ready, tip this into the flour and sugar mix along with the beaten egg and melted butter, and stir with a wooden spoon to bring together.

Knead with a dough hook for 7–8 minutes, until smooth and springy, or with your hands for 10 minutes, adding a little more flour as needed to get a workable dough.

Drain the brandy from the fruit, and carefully fold the fruit into the dough. Form it into a ball, then cover and leave to rise for 2 hours, or until doubled in size.

Punch down the dough, then start your shaping. As shaping stollen is a little hard to describe, you can head to my website for a video where I show you how to do it (see page 236).

Alternatively, shape the dough into a large oval – around 25cm long. Use a rolling pin to make a lengthways deep indentation, almost to your work surface, along one third of the long end of the oval. Roll your marzipan into a long log, and place it in the indentation. Use the rolling pin to make a shallower indentation in the middle of the remaining two-thirds of the stollen, then fold the side with the marzipan over so that the marzipan is completely enclosed – you should have a hump exactly in the middle so a cross section would look like a camel's back – pat down around the hump with your rolling pin to further define it.

Let the dough rise for 1 hour at room temperature, then transfer to a oven preheated to 180°C fan/200°C/gas 6 and bake for 25–30 minutes, until golden brown and risen.

Brush over the melted butter and sift over icing sugar to taste, then let the stollen cool on a wire rack. Once cool, you can let it mature for a week in an airtight container, but I find this easier said than done.

See page 212 for reference.

DATE & WALNUT RUGELACH

If there is one recipe in this book that I'd make on a weekly rotation, it's these beautifully tender, flaky crescent biscuits, known as rugelach. Traditionally baked for Hannukah, there are any number of fillings you can use – jam, Nutella, other types of toasted nut – but I like this one with blitzed dates and toasted walnuts best.

Makes:	32 biscuits
Prep:	15 minutes, + 2½ hours chilling
Cook:	20–25 minutes

100g walnuts
200g cold cubed butter
200g cold cream cheese
50g caster sugar
300g plain flour
200g soft pitted dates
1 medium free-range egg, beaten
Demerara sugar, to scatter

Preheat the oven to 160°C fan/180°C/gas 4, and toast the walnuts for 10 minutes. Set aside.

Tip the butter, cream cheese, caster sugar and plain flour into a food processor and blitz until it comes together as a slightly sticky dough. Remove from the processor, dust liberally with flour and divide into two flattish discs. Alternatively, you can use your fingertips to work the butter and cream cheese into the flour and sugar, before bringing together into two discs as above.

Wrap the discs in clingfilm or place in small bags, and transfer to the fridge to chill for 2 hours.

Meanwhile, blitz the walnuts with the dates in the food processor or in a high-speed blender until you have a thick paste. Set aside.

Once the dough has chilled, roll out the first disc on a cold floured surface to the size of a dinner plate. Scatter half the date and walnut mixture evenly over the dough, leaving a 2.5cm border around the edges of the pastry.

Cut the pastry as if slicing a pizza into 16 long wedges, then roll each wedge up, starting at the largest end. (This is easier viewed than described, so you can head to my website for a video if you wish – see page 236.)

Transfer the rolled biscuits to a lined baking sheet, and brush with the beaten egg. Scatter with demerara sugar, and return to the fridge to chill for 20 minutes. Repeat with the remaining dough and filling (though both freeze well for future baking).

When you're ready to cook, preheat the oven to 180°C fan/200°C/gas 6. Bake the rugelach for 20–25 minutes, until golden brown, and serve warm or at room temperature.

Any leftovers will keep well in an airtight container for 2–3 days (unless you invite me around, in which case they'll be gone within minutes).

See page 213 for reference.

FOR GLUTEN-FREE: replace the plain flour with gluten-free plain flour.

TARTA DE SANTIAGO

This delicious almond cake originates in Galicia, where to be called a proper Tarta de Santiago the proportions of the ingredients must meet the standards of the Consello Regulador – no less than 33% almonds, 33% sugar and 25% eggs. I love this sort of precision when baking – for an authentic finish, you can cut out a St James cross from an online template, and use it as a stencil before decorating the cake with icing sugar.

Serves: 8
Prep: 10 minutes
Cook: 40 minutes

4 medium free-range eggs
250g caster sugar
250g ground almonds
1 lemon, zest only
½ teaspoon ground cinnamon
Icing sugar, to dust

Preheat the oven to 160°C fan/180°C/gas 4. Butter and line a 20cm round cake tin and set aside.

Using a freestanding or hand-held electric whisk, beat the eggs and caster sugar until light, pale and foamy – there's no other raising agent in this cake, so it's important to beat in as much air as possible. This will take about 5 minutes.

Very gently fold in the ground almonds a few tablespoons at a time, along with the lemon zest and ground cinnamon. Spoon the batter into the lined cake tin, then transfer to the oven and bake for 40 minutes, until golden brown and firm on top.

Let the cake cool in its tin before unmoulding and placing on a wire rack.

If using a decorative stencil, place it in the middle of the cake and dust with icing sugar, carefully removing the stencil afterwards.

Serve warm or at room temperature. Leftovers will keep well in an airtight container for 2–3 days.

COCONUT BURFI

These are the sweets of my childhood, made every year for Diwali. While I haven't a sufficient sweet tooth for many Indian desserts, these are the exception (OK – along with jalebi and rasmalai). Think of these as a toffee-ish coconut fudge, with a soft, melting texture – really easy to make, even quicker to disappear.

Makes: around 20 pieces
Prep: 5 minutes
Cook: 10 minutes
+ 40 minutes setting

250g unsweetened desiccated coconut
1 x standard tin of condensed milk
A handful of coconut flakes

Put the coconut into a heavy-based saucepan along with the condensed milk. Using a wooden spoon, stir continuously over a low heat for about 7–10 minutes – the mixture will thicken and get a little hard to stir, so enlist another pair of hands if you need them – you'll know when it's done, as it will start to get glossy and come away cleanly from the sides of the pan.

Tip the mixture out into a lightly buttered 25cm shallow round tin, and flatten with the back of a metal tablespoon to just over 5mm thick. Scatter over the coconut flakes, and gently press them down into the surface.

Let the burfi cool for 10 minutes before scoring into diamond shapes, and for a further 30 minutes before cutting the shapes out.

These are lovely slightly warm, but will keep well once cooled in an airtight container for up to a week.

GLUTEN-FREE, VEGAN & DIABETIC-FRIENDLY RECIPES

OR EASY ADAPTATIONS

CONVERSION TABLE	NATURALLY			EASILY CONVERTIBLE		
	GLUTEN-FREE	VEGAN	DIABETIC-FRIENDLY	GLUTEN-FREE	VEGAN	DIABETIC-FRIENDLY
TRAYBAKES						
18 Cherry & almond cake				Yes		
20 Chocolate-lime truffle cake						Yes
22 Coconut & mango yogurt cake				Yes		Yes
24 Marmalade coffee cake						Yes
26 Orange & hazelnut cake				Yes		Yes
28 Apple & pine nut cake				Yes		Yes
30 Spiced carrot & coconut cake	Yes					
MUFFIN TINS						
38 Blackberry cream cheese muffins					Yes	Yes
40 Intense chocolate salted caramel muffins					Yes	Yes
42 Raspberry, lemon & hazelnut crumble muffins						
44 Peanut butter, raspberry & banana muffins		Yes				
46 Black pepper, cheddar & sage muffins			Yes	Yes		
48 Goat's cheese, fig & basil muffins				Yes		Yes
50 Roasted tomato, ricotta & thyme muffins			Yes	Yes		
52 Chilli-spiked halloumi & courgette muffins			Yes	Yes		
LOAF TINS						
60 Vanilla & bay loaf				Yes		Yes
62 Sticky date gingerbread			Yes			
64 Chocolate & rosemary loaf						Yes
66 Saffron & orange banana bread		Yes				
68 Marzipan, lemon & cardamom loaf				Yes		
70 Afternoon tea loaf				Yes		Yes
BROWNIES						
78 Chocolate passionfruit brownies	Yes					Yes
80 Caramel pecan brownies	Yes					
82 Stem ginger, cherry & almond brownies	Yes					
84 Rhubarb & custard blondies				Yes		
86 Pistachio & date brownies	Yes		Yes			
88 Baked mascarpone, cherry & walnut brownies	Yes					

CONVERSION TABLE

		NATURALLY			EASILY CONVERTIBLE		
		GLUTEN-FREE	VEGAN	DIABETIC-FRIENDLY	GLUTEN-FREE	VEGAN	DIABETIC-FRIENDLY
COOKIES							
96	Salted chocolate chip cookies		Yes		Yes		Yes
98	Chocolate, coconut & brazil nut cookies		Yes		Yes		Yes
100	Old-fashioned fruit & nut cookies		Yes		Yes		Yes
102	Fig, fennel & orange cookies		Yes		Yes		Yes
104	Triple ginger biscuits		Yes		Yes		Yes
106	Spelt, cheddar & caraway biscuits			Yes			
CRUMBLES, TARTS & COBBLERS							
114	Banoffee chocolate tarts				Yes		
116	Plum, cherry & cinnamon cobbler						
118	Peach, ginger & almond crumble				Yes		
120	Rhubarb & vanilla tart				Yes		
122	Pear, blackberry & cardamom crumble				Yes		
124	Apple, cheddar & clove galette						
BREAD & BUTTER PUDDINGS							
130	Chocolate bread & butter pudding				Yes		
132	Coffee & walnut croissant pudding				Yes		
134	Amaretto panettone bread & butter pudding						
136	Orange chocolate chip bread & butter pudding				Yes		
138	Sticky toffee brioche pudding			Yes			
140	Pistachio pain au chocolat pudding				Yes		
MINIMAL BAKING							
146	Marshmallow, peanut & chocolate cornflake cups						
148	Chocolate, cherry & pistachio fridge cake				Yes	Yes	
150	Mini's peanut butter cups	Yes	Yes				Yes
152	Maple pecan flapjacks				Yes		
154	Cranberry almond flapjacks		Yes		Yes		
156	Chocolate lemon mascarpone cheesecake				Yes		

CONVERSION TABLE

		NATURALLY			EASILY CONVERTIBLE		
		Gluten-free	Vegan	Diabetic-friendly	Gluten-free	Vegan	Diabetic-friendly
CUPCAKES							
162	Lavender cupcakes				Yes		
164	Rose & pistachio cupcakes	Yes					
166	Black forest cupcakes						
168	Rosemary lemon curd cupcakes				Yes		
170	Pineapple & coconut cupcakes	Yes					
172	Raspberry bakewell cupcakes	Yes					
DOUGH							
182	Rainbow iced buns					Yes	
184	Chocolate, almond & raisin jumble bread					Yes	Yes
186	Cardamom & cinnamon knots					Yes	Yes
188	Caramel apple chelsea buns						
190	Stuffed rosemary & roasted garlic dough balls					Yes	Yes
192	Camembert dipping wheel					Yes	Yes
194	Parmesan & Parma ham buns						Yes
196	Spiced focaccia with roasted with roasted butternut squash		Yes				
HIGH DAYS & HOLIDAYS							
AROUND THE WORLD							
204	Zoe's Granny's fruit cake						
206	Chocolate, clementine & stem ginger puddings						
208	Iced & spiced gingerbread				Yes		
210	Marzipan stollen						
214	Date & walnut rugelach				Yes		
216	Tarta de Santiago	Yes					
218	Coconut burfi	Yes					

INFORMATION FOR DIABETICS		NUTRITION PER RECIPE				RECOMMENDED DIABETIC SERVING SIZE	
		Nutrient	Full recipe (grams)	Servings	Full serving (grams)	Diabetic servings	Full serving (grams)
20	Chocolate-lime truffle cake	Carbohydrates / of which sugars / of which polyols	339 / 124 / 90	8	42 / 16 / 11	16	21 / 8 / 6
22	Coconut & mango yogurt cake	Carbohydrates / of which sugars / of which polyols	172 / 62 / 70	8	22 / 8 / 9	16	11 / 4 / 4
24	Marmalade coffee cake	Carbohydrates / of which sugars / of which polyols	275 / 7 / 87	8	34 / 1 / 11	16	17 / 0 / 5
26	Orange & hazelnut cake	Carbohydrates / of which sugars / of which polyols	291 / 118 / 78	8	36 / 15 / 10	16	18 / 7 / 5
28	Apple & pine nut cake	Carbohydrates / of which sugars / of which polyols	229 / 45 / 78	8	29 / 6 / 10	16	14 / 3 / 5
38	Blackberry cream cheese muffins	Carbohydrates / of which sugars	315 / 122	12	26 / 10	Serving as suggestion in recipe	
40	Intense chocolate salted caramel muffins	Carbohydrates / of which sugars / of which polyols	371 / 148 / 45	12	31 / 12 / 4	16	23 / 9 / 3
46	Black pepper, cheddar & sage muffins	Carbohydrates / of which sugars	193 / 15	12	16 / 1	Serving as suggestion in recipe	
48	Goat's cheese, fig & basil muffins	Carbohydrates / of which sugars	222 / 43	12	19 / 4	Serving as suggestion in recipe	
50	Roasted tomato, ricotta & thyme muffins	Carbohydrates / of which sugars	193 / 19	12	16 / 2	Serving as suggestion in recipe	
52	Chilli-spiked halloumi & courgette muffins	Carbohydrates / of which sugars	194 / 16	12	16 / 1	Serving as suggestion in recipe	
60	Vanilla & bay loaf	Carbohydrates / of which sugars / of which polyols	207 / 6 / 80	8	26 / 1 / 10	Serving as suggestion in recipe	
62	Sticky date gingerbread	Carbohydrates / of which sugars	354 / 210	8	44 / 26	16	22 / 13
64	Chocolate & rosemary loaf	Carbohydrates / of which sugars / of which polyols	327 / 126 / 45	8	41 / 16 / 6	16	20 / 8 / 3
70	Afternoon tea loaf	Carbohydrates / of which sugars	344 / 184	8	43 / 23	16	21 / 11
78	Chocolate passionfruit brownies	Carbohydrates / of which sugars / of which polyols	156 / 106 / 23	8	19 / 13 / 3	Serving as suggestion in recipe	
86	Pistachio & date brownies	Carbohydrates / of which sugars / of which polyols	183 / 125 / 23	8	23 / 16 / 3	Serving as suggestion in recipe	
96	Salted chocolate chip cookies	Carbohydrates / of which sugars / of which polyols	395 / 117 / 45	12–15	33 / 10 / 4	16	25 / 7 / 3
98	Chocolate, coconut & brazil nut cookies	Carbohydrates / of which sugars / of which polyols	353 / 118 / 23	12–15	29 / 10 / 2	16	22 / 7 / 1
100	Old-fashioned fruit & nut cookies	Carbohydrates / of which sugars / of which polyols	470 / 183 / 45	12–15	29 / 11 / 3	Serving as suggestion in recipe	
102	Fig, fennel & orange cookies	Carbohydrates / of which sugars	454 / 221	12–15	38 / 18	18	25 / 12
104	Triple ginger biscuits	Carbohydrates / of which sugars	348 / 117	12–15	29 / 10	16	22 / 7
106	Spelt, cheddar & caraway biscuits	Carbohydrates / of which sugars	73 / 2	20	4 / 0	Serving as suggestion in recipe	
138	Sticky toffee brioche pudding	Carbohydrates / of which sugars	262 / 96	6	44 / 16	16	22 / 8
150	Mini's peanut butter cups	Carbohydrates / of which sugars	45 / 5	12	4 / 0	Serving as suggestion in recipe	
179	Sweet diabetic dough	Carbohydrates / of which sugars / of which polyols	250 / 9 / 15	1	250 / 9 / 15	Serving as suggestion in recipe	
179	Savoury diabetic dough	Carbohydrates / of which sugars	228 / 2	1	228 / 2	Serving as suggestion in recipe	
184	Chocolate, almond & raisin jumble bread	Carbohydrates / of which sugars / of which polyols	311 / 42 / 38	8	39 / 5 / 5	Serving as suggestion in recipe	
186	Cardamon & cinnamon knots	Carbohydrates / of which sugars / of which polyols	292 / 42 / 15	13–16	18 / 3 / 1	Serving as suggestion in recipe	
190	Stuffed rosemary & garlic dough balls	Carbohydrates / of which sugars	238 / 3	16	15 / 0	Serving as suggestion in recipe	
192	Camembert dipping wheel	Carbohydrates / of which sugars	232 / 3	4	58 / 1	8	29 / 0
194	Parmesan & Parma ham buns	Carbohydrates / of which sugars	424 / 2	16	26 / 0	Serving as suggestion in recipe	

INDEX

ABOUT THE AUTHOR

Rukmini Iyer is the bestselling author of the *Roasting Tin* series. She is a recipe writer, food stylist and formerly a lawyer. She loves creating delicious and easy recipes with minimum fuss and maximum flavour. Rukmini believes family dinners are an integral part of the day and is passionate about helping people make it possible.

Rukmini grew up making fairy cakes, flapjacks and meringues with her mother, graduating to more elaborate bakes from the family collection of baking and patisserie books. She fell in with a group of like-minded friends at university, where there were almost always home-made cakes or cookies to go with pots of tea at their student flat. After a career change from the law, Rukmini retrained in food, working in a Michelin-starred pastry kitchen for a summer before starting a career as a food stylist. Surrounded by food all day on photo-shoots, she noticed the meals she made at home grew simpler, often just in one tin, and that there were ways of packing in flavour and interest into dishes with an absolute minimum of effort – this became the inspiration for the best-selling *Roasting Tin* series.

As well as writing cookbooks, Rukmini styles and writes recipes for numerous brands and publications, including Waitrose, *The Guardian* and Fortnum & Mason. When not working with food, she can usually be found walking her beautiful border collie Pepper by the riverside in East London, entertaining at home or filling her balcony and flat with more plants than they can hold. Rukmini runs an occasional series of supper clubs for charities including Oxfam and Women's Aid.

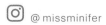 @ missminifer    @ missminifer

For all recipe videos, head to www.rukmini-iyer.com/videos.

ACKNOWLEDGEMENTS

My thanks to the incredible team at Square Peg and Vintage for their work on this book. In particular I'd like to thank Mireille Harper and Tamsin English, editors of dreams, Sarah Bennie, Kate Neilan and Lucie Cuthbertson-Twiggs for brilliant PR and marketing and to Shabana Cho for facilitating a smooth production process. Thanks to Felicity Blunt for sound advice and fantastic chat and to Jennifer Martin for providing the nutritional information for the book.

Pene Parker, you took the brief 'let's make this book look as edible as a Ladurée macaron' and have designed the most stunning book we've worked on to date. David Loftus, your photography as ever has made the book what it is, thank you for such wonderful pictures.

Jo Jackson, thank you for helping bake so many of the recipes and keeping me on track while shooting, I couldn't have done it and stayed sane without you. Thanks to Falcon Enamelware for many of the tins used in the photography.

Very lucky to have the crack recipe testing team of Pippa Leon and Jo Jackson on the recipes, again along with invaluable at-home testing from Christine Beck, Danielle Adams, Emma Drage, Laura Hutchinson, Rosie Breckner and not least Parvati Iyer (Mum!) – your suggestions and amends were as always thoughtful and helpful – thank you.

Dad, I am sorry you aren't able to eat so many of the foods you enjoy but thanks to Mum's determination and creativity we now know how to adapt sweet recipes in a healthy way for you. Maybe we should buy shares in date syrup? Moma, thanks for teaching me how to bake and encouraging early experiments in the kitchen, and Padz; you are a ridic support team, in return I promise not to try to feed you cake unless v small and from Gail's.

TY, I am sorry that eating our way through this book temporarily blurred our waistlines. Pepper and I love you very much (though she may be angling for a cheddar penguin).

10 9 8 7 6 5 4 3 2 1

Square Peg, an imprint of Vintage,
Penguin Random House UK
One Embassy Gardens,
8 Viaduct Gardens, London, SW11 7BW

Square Peg is part of the Penguin Random House group
of companies whose addresses can be found at:
global.penguinrandomhouse.com.

Penguin
Random House
UK

First published by Square Peg in 2021
Penguin.co.uk/vintage

A CIP catalogue record for this book is available
from the British Library
ISBN 9781529110432

Art direction, design and prop styling by Pene Parker
Photography by David Loftus
Food styling by Rukmini Iyer
Food styling assistance by Jo Jackson
Recipe testing by Pippa Leon and Jo Jackson
Nutritional advice by Jennifer Martin

Printed and bound in Italy by L.E.G.O. S.p.A.

Penguin Random House is committed to a sustainable future
for our business, our readers and our planet.
This book is made from Forest Stewardship Council® certified paper.

AVAILABLE NOW